An Account of King's College-Chapel, in Cambridge; (embellished With a Plate of the Chapel

An ACCOUNT of
KING's COLLEGE-CHAPEL,
In CAMBRIDGE;

(Embellifhed with a Plate of the *Chapel* and a Print of the *Author* executed by a Gentleman of the Univerfity)

Including a Character of HENRY VI.

And a fhort Hiftory of the Foundation of his two Colleges,
KING's and ETON

And containing, though briefly, the following Articles ·

I An Extract of the Founder's Will, relating to the finifhing of the Chapel; (with a Digreffion concerning the intended College)

II. A particular Relation of the Progrefs of that Edifice, under the Reigns of thofe Kings who contributed to complete it

III. The original Ufe of the Veftries on each Side of the Building.— Some very ancient Infcriptions on the Tomb-ftones within them.— A remarkable Epitaph

IV An accurate Defcription of whatever is worthy of Notice within the Chapel —Wonderful Structure of the Stone-Roof. which occafions a Mention of the original Secret of Free-Mafons, and fome few Particulars concerning that Society. With

V. A FULL Explanation of all the curious Paintings on the Windows in the Courfe of which is fhewn the Correfpondence between the hiftorical Paintings drawn from the Old Teftament and thofe taken from the New

To which is added,

A Lift of all the Provofts, Bifhops, Statefmen, learned Writers, Martyrs and Confeffors, who were formerly Members of KING's College, extracted partly from Fuller's Church-Hiftory of Britain —The Author's Apology and grateful Acknowledgments to his Subfcribers — With Copies of feveral ancient Indentures, fetting forth an Account of many different Sums of Money expended on finifhing and glazing the Chapel.—Each particular Beauty of the Windows remarked

By HENRY MALDEN, Chapel-Clerk.

——— above! around!
Behold where e'er this penfile quarry's found,
Or fwelling into vaulted roofs it's weight,
Or fhooting columns into Gothic ftate,
Where e'er this fane extends it's lofty frame,
Behold the monument to HENRY's name.

Dodfley's Poems, Vol. VII.

CAMBRIDGE,
Printed for the AUTHOR, by FLETCHER and HODSON;
And fold by J Woodyer, T. and J. Merrill, R. Matthews, J Paris, Fletcher and Hoofon, and by the Author, at the Sign of the Hat, in the Butcher-Row, Cambridge, J Beecroft, S. Crowder, J Johnfon and Co in Pater-nofter row, J. Rivington, St. Paul's Church yard, B White, Fleet-ftreet, T Payne, Mews, and J Dodfley, Pall mall, London, J Pote, at Eton, J Blakeney, at Windfor, and by all the Bookfellers in Town and Country. 1769.

To the PUBLIC.

THOUGH Endeavours, however imperfect, have not been wanting to render this Work in some degree entertaining, yet it may not be improper to acquaint the Public, that it's Author, from the diftrefs of his family, claims the peculiar pity and protection of every tender and compaf fionate chriftian.

For if the confideration of a numerous family, of a Wife difordered in her mind, of a Hufband relieving (or at leaft endeavouring to relieve) her under that calamity, by means that far exceed the limits of a fcanty maintenance, and thereby involving himfelf in neceffitous circumftances, demands a kind and bountiful affiftance; then will every one, who has a feeling heart, contribute largely and liberally to this Author's fupport. It is fincerely wifhed, that the fame fpirit of beneficence, which has hitherto promoted the fale of the following fheets, even beyond his higheft expectation, may yet recommend them to others that, by fuch means, the hand of Charity may univerfally be extended for his relief; and that he may experience the effects of that generofity, which finds the nobleft rewards in it's own exertion.

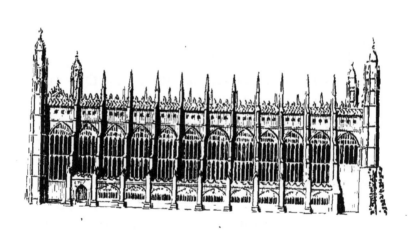

KING'S COLLEGE CHAPEL.

A

TABLE of CONTENTS;

Intended chiefly for thofe, who fhall make ufe of the Book while they are furveying the Chapel.

. N is placed for Note

A 2   Anne

An ACCOUNT of

KING's COLLEGE-CHAPEL,

IN

CAMBRIDGE.

HENRY VI. the Founder of King's College, was proclaimed (1422) while yet in his cradle, King of England; and in the eighth year of his age, crowned and acknowledged King of France at Paris.

THIS Prince, although inferior to his illustrious father (Henry V.) in the glory of military enterprises, yet, from an innocence and purity of manners, lays claim to no small share of our esteem and admiration. Mild and equable in his temper, just and upright in his conduct, liberal in the encouragement of learning, zealous in the advancement of religion, he was qualified, while alive, to gain the affections of his people, and is intitled, after death, to a character which does an honour to his memory. The only reproach, to which his actions have exposed him, is an irresolute and fearful disposition: a defect, over which Benevolence will cast a veil, imputing it to an excess of humanity, rather than to a want of magnanimity. An imperfection of such a nature may be the object of our concern, but not our censure.

SENSIBLE

SENSIBLE of the rough, uncultivated genius of his nation, HENRY eftablifhed in his kingdom feats of erudition, enriched them with ample endowments, and diftinguifhed them by privileges and immunities · thus inviting his fubjects to forfake their ignorance and barbarifm, and reform their turbulent and licentious manners   A more effectual expedient he could not have employed for the patronage of religion and letters, nor have left a more magnificent monument of himfelf for the ornament of fucceeding ages.

THE eftablifhment of literary foundations, the fupport and tutelage of a Monarch, fenfibly introduced a change on the face of learning, and added ftrength and fpirit to it's drooping caufe   Encouraged by this illuftrious perfonage, and allured by an ambition to excel, men of parts and capacity entertained a fondnefs for literature, and purfued it with unwearied diligence   The ftudy of the ancient languages began to be held in great eftimation, an elegance in compofition was gradually introduced, and, in a due courfe of years a refined tafte for poetry and eloquence was diffufed throughout all ranks of writers

WHOEVER fhall fearch the annals of preceding centuries, will find his country indebted to HENRY's munificence for many of her moft fagacious ftatefmen, confummate orators, and admired writers. who, unlefs raifed and protected by his bounty, had moft probably, from a meannefs of education, lived and died in ignorance and obfcurity   And who but beholds with an unfeigned fatisfaction that height of glory, to which the two renowned Colleges of this Prince's inftitution, KINGS and ETON, have, in the prefent age, attained, where the talents of the ingenious have never paffed unknown and unrewarded ?

NOT lefs, therefore, have been the advantages derived from thefe inftitutions, than were intended by the pious liberality of their Founder   which great work he began to take in hand, when he was yet but in the nineteenth year of his age and reign.

ETON

ETON-COLLEGE, a place peculiarly fitted for a calm, contemplative retirement, though it was founded somewhat later than KING's, shall have the first place in my account of the two societies, that I may afterward pursue the history of KING's without interruption.

THIS account (as it contains something curious) I shall set down in the very words of Fuller, to whom the Reader will perceive I am under no small obligation for materials in the ensuing pages.

" THE King soon after (1446) founded EATON
" Colledg, and called it *The King's College, of our*
" *Lady,* (the Virgin Mary) *of Eaton, beside Windsor.*—
" Indeed it was high time some school should be
" founded, considering how low Grammer-Learning
" ran then in the land, as may appear by the follow-
" ing verses made for King HENRY the Founder, as
" good no doubt as the generality of that age did af-
" ford, though (scarce deserving translation) so that
" the worst scholar in EATON Colledg, that can make
" a verse, can make a better.

' *Luce tua qui natus erat, Nicolae, sacer Rex*
    ' Henricus Sextus *hoc stabilivit opus.*
' *Unctum qui lapidem postquam ponebat in Eaton*
    ' *Hunc fixit, clerum commemorando suum.**

                     ' *Afsterant*

---

* From these two lines some are led to determine the subject of this piece of poetry, *viz* the foundation of KING's College-Chapel Nor is such decision without reason. For the very words in this copy of verses tell us—that they were composed on laying the first stone of some building in 1446. which was the year in which HENRY VI. granted the College a stone-quarry in Yorkshire for building their Chapel Now this grant was made March 4, 1446, and it is not improbable but that, within four or five months after a concession of such grant, the foundation of the Chapel was laid Allowing then this for a truth, the first stone of KING's College-Chapel was laid on the feast of St. James, July 25, 1446.

' *Aſtiterant illi tunc Pontifices in honorem*
' *Actus ſolennis regis et Eccleſiæ.*
' *Ex Orientali** ſi bis ſeptem pedotentam*
' *Menſurare velis, invenies lapidem;*
' *In feſto ſancti Jacobi ſanctam ſtabilivit*
' *Hic unctam Petram regia ſacra manus.*

' *Annis M CCCC ſexto quater Xque,*
' *Regis et H. Regni quinto jungendo vicena.*

" Devout King HENRY of that name the ſixt,
" Born (Nic'las) on thy day this building fixt,
" In EATON having plac'd a ſtone anointed
" In ſign, it for the Clergy was appointed
" His Prelates then were preſent, ſo the more
" To honour the King's acts and holy chore.
" From Eaſtern midſt, whereof juſt fourteen feet
" If any meaſure, they this ſtone ſhall meet,
" On holy James his day, the ſacred hand
" Of Royal HENRY caus'd this ſtone to ſtand

" M. four C:s fourty ſix ſince Chriſt was born,
" When H. the Crown twenty-five years† had worn.

" THIS Colledg conſiſteth of one Provoſt, ſeven
" Fellows, two Schoolmaſters,‡ with ſeventy King's
" Scholars, beſides many Oppidanes,** maintained
" there at the coſt of their friends, ſo that was EATON
" removed into Germany, it would no longer be ac
" counted one of the *Scholæ*, but *Gymnaſia*, a middle
" terme betwixt a *School*, and an *Univerſity* The
" Provoſtſhip of EATON is accounted one of the
" gentileſt, and intireſt preferments in England, the
" Provoſt thereof, being provided for in all particu
" lars, to the very point of his hoſe (my deſire is one
                                        " tag

---

* *Medio.*
† *Viz* current, otherwiſe but twenty-four complete.
‡ Beſides an Upper and Lower-Maſter there are, at this
time, ten Aſſiſtant-Maſters
** The number of King's Scholars and Oppidans is at
preſent about five hundred.

" tag of them may not be diminished) and as a plea-
" fant Courtier told King Henry the Eighth, ' an
' hundred pound a year more than enough ' How
" true this is I know not; this I know, if some
" Courtiers were to stint the *enough* of Clergymen,
" even the most industrious of them should (with So-
" lomon's* slothful man) have *poverty enough.*

" THIS EATON is a Nursery † to KING's Colledg
" in CAMBRIDG. All that I will add, is, to wish,
" that the prime scholars in this school may annually
" be chosen to the University, and when chosen,
" their places may fall accordingly, not by the *death*
" of those in KING's Colledg, but their advancement
" to better preferment in the Church and Common-
" wealth "

IF we look back awhile, to trace KING's College
to it's origin, we shall find it but mean in it's first insti-
tution (1441) having only a Rector and twelve Scholars. But, before the expiration of two years from
this foundation, HENRY entirely changed it's form,
dedicating it to the Virgin Mary and St. Nicholas, ‡ and
bestowing on it a most ample endowment: at which
time

---

* Prov. xxviii. 19.

† It is with great propriety, that Fuller calls this school a
Nurfery to KING's College for, from among the seventy
scholars of the foundation, and no others, those of the upper
class are, as vacant Fellowships require, preferred to KING's
College. There they have Scholarships, as soon as they are
admitted, and three years after their admission, Fellowships.

‡ In ancient times there stood a church dedicated to Saint
Nicholas within the compass of the College
St Nicholas' day (December 6) was the birth-day of HEN-
RY VI as appears both from his Charter granted to KING's
College, and the verses quoted above.
The glorious Confessor St. Nicholas (as he is usually called)
was Bishop of Myra, in Lycia, a province of Asia.

time (1443) he placed therein a Provoft, feventy*
Fellows and Scholars, ten Conducts, fixteen Chorifters and a Mafter over them, who is likewife the
Organift, fix fingirg Clerks, fixteen fervants to the
College, befides twelve Servitors † to the Senior Fel
lows, and fix poor Scholars, † amounting in all to an
hundred and thirty-one; and called it *The King's College of our Lady, and Saint Nicholas, in Cambridge*

SCARCELY had he laid the foundation of his College, when he began to build for it the Chapel,
(which is chiefly the fubject of thefe pages) juftly
efteemed one of the moft magnificent Gothic ftruc
tures in the whole world   Conformable to the gran
deur of which he intended to have built the College
but, being involved in the miferies of a civil war
with the houfe of York, he was prevented from
completing his defign   At length, after a feries of
public misfortunes, and many tedious confinements in
the Tower of London, he was murdered, (1471) ac
cording to the hiftorians of that age, by the Duke of
Gloucefter's ‡ own hands.

THUS did this unfortunate Prince leave the College
as well as the Chapel, to be finifhed at the expence of
fucceeding Kings.

HENRY, however, even amidft all his calamities,
though he was waging a perpetual war, which
threaten, d his government, and perhaps his life, with
an

---

* It is obfervable, that there are *feventy* Scholars and Fellows at KING's, and *feventy* Scholars at ETON.   On the firft
foundation likewife of KING's College, we find *twelve* Scho
lars with a Mafter compofing the Society   Now that thefe
numbers, in preference to all others, were made choice of
in allufion to Chrift's *feventy* Difciples and *twelve* Apoftles,
no one, I fuppofe, ever made a doubt, who was acquainted
with the fuperftitious manners of the age, in which the
Founder lived

† The Servitors and poor Scholars are not of the Foundation

‡ Afterwards Richard III

an hourly diffolution, was not unmindful of the work
he had undertaken . as appears by the following extract of his Will.

"   As touching the dimenfions of the Church of
" my faid College, of our Lady and St Nicholas of
" CAMBRIDGE, I have devifed and appointed, that
" the fame Church fhall contain in length 288 foot
" of affife, without any ifles, and all of the widenefs
" of 40 foot, and the length of the fame Church,
" from the Weft end unto the altars at the Choir
" door, fhall contain 120 foot, and from the Pro-
" voft's Stall unto the Greece *(that is, to the fartheft
part of the prefent Stalls)* call'd *Gradus Chori*, 90 foot,
" for 36 Stalls on either fide of the faid Choir, an-
" fwering to 70 Fellows, and 10 Priefts Conducts,
" which muft be *de prima forma* and from the faid
" Stalls unto the Eaft end of the faid Church 22 foot
" of affife. Alfo a Reredoffe bearing the Rood-
" loft,* *(by which, I fuppofe, is meant fomething of the
fame kind with the prefent Organ-loft)* departing the
" Choir and the body of the Church, containing in
" length 40 foot, and in breadth 14 foot.   The Walls
" of the fame Church to be in height 90 foot, im-
" batteled, vaulted, and chareroofed, fufficiently but-
" tereffed, and every Butterefs fixed with Finials · *(or
" Pinnacles)* And in the Eaft end of the fame Church
" fhall be a Window of 9 Days, *(or Lights)* and be-
" twixt every of the fame Buttereffes in the body of
" the Church, on both fides of the faid Church, a
" Clofet with an Altar therein, containing in length
" 20 foot, and in breadth 10 foot, vaulted and fi-
" nifhed under the Soyle of the Ifle Windows, and
" the pavement of the Church, *(that is, the Ante-Cha-
" pel)* to be enhanced four foot above the ground
" without, and the height of the pavement of the
" Choir one foot and a half above the pavement of
" the

---

* On the Roodloft in Roman Catholic churches is fixed a
crofs and within the fame are repofited all holy relicks

" the Church; and the pavement of the Altar three
" foot above that, and on the North fide of the
" Choir a Veftry containing in length 50 foot, and
" in breadth 22 foot, departed into two houfes be-
" neath, and two houfes above, which fhall contain
" in height 22 foot in all, with an entry from the
" Choir vaulted, &c "*

HE then proceeds to defcribe the dimenfions of the
College he intended to build, which (had he ever completed his defign) would have confifted chiefly of one
large Square, on the North of which would have ftood
the Chapel. Two fides of this Square would have
joined the Chapel: the South fide whereof towards
the Eaft yet remains unfinifhed ‡ (from whence may be
feen the intended height of the Building) From this
end of the Chapel may be difcovered, a little underneath the furface of the ground, a foundation † by
tracing which may eafily be perceived the length of
two fides of the intended Square But of the length it is
eafy to form a judgment from the prefent New Building, the nobleft modern ftructure in the Univerfity

CONCERNING the College, the following words
are delivered down to us in Stow's Chronicle, of the
edition of 1631.

" I fuppofe that if the reft of the Houfe (meaning
the College) had proceeded according to the Chapel al-
" ready finifhed, as his (that is, the Founder's) full in-
" tent and meaning was, the like College could fcarce
" have been found again in any chriftian land. This
                                              " College

---

* The Chapel is built, in every refpect, nearly according
to thefe directions in the Will

‡ See the Plate of the Chapel, in which the unfinifhed
work is reprefented under the Half-Window.

† There is yet remaining part of a wall built for the Eaft
fide of the intended Square within which may be perceived
fome few frames or cafes of ftone, defigned for fire-places —
In that end of the wall, which is neareft the Chapel, remains a
large iron hinge, on which it was intended that a gate fhould
have been hung, opening towards Trumpington-ftreet

" College was begun in his time, and finished so far,
" that in the year 1443, which was the 23d of his
" reign, the cemitery or church-yard, the altar, &c.
" as the manner was, were confecrated by the Bishops
" of Salisbury and Lincoln."—See note p. 32.

FULLER likewife, in his Church-Hiftory, fpeaks of
it in the following manner.

" THE whole College was intended conformable
" to the Chapel: but the untimely death (or rather
" depofing) of King HENRY the Sixth hindred the
" fame   Thus foundations partake of their founder's
" intereft, and flourifh or fade together.   Yea, that
" mean quadrant (almoft all the College extant at
" this day) was at firft defigned only for the Cho-
" rifters "*

THE whole of even this fmall Court (two fides of
which only contain apartments for the College) is not
finifhed uniformly ; as any one may difcover by ob-
ferving the upper part of one half of the Weft fide of
the Court

OVER the Weft gate, (without this old Building)
and on the North fide of it, are to be feen two Rofes,
and a fmall figure of a Hand   all which are carved
with uncommon art †—But to return to my fubject.

How

---

* Fuller was mifinformed in this piece of hiftory relating
to the old Court . for it was not built for the Chorifters, but
for the Rector and twelve Scholars placed in the College at
it's firft inftitution , at which time the Founder dedicated it
to St Nicholas, and erected for it a fmall Chapel on that fpot
where the Combination-room, and the firft room on the right,
as you enter the Court, now ftand.

† On the Weft fide, and near the battlements of the Old
Building, are fixed fome grotefque heads, each having a leaden
pipe in it's mouth ——An indelicate metaphor of the poet
Manilius has given occafion to a mention of thefe in Fitzof-
borne's Letters   For fpeaking of unpardonable defects both
of tafte and judgment in fome writers, in the application of
their metaphors, he introduces the following paffage.

" The poet Manilius feems to have raifed an image of the
" fame

How far the Chapel was advanced at the Founder's
death, is uncertain.   But be this as it may, there needs
no fcruple to aſſert, that the foundation of the far
greater part of this majeſtic ſtructure was then little
more than aiſed above the ground.   For the height to
which it was, in ſome parts, carried, is ſuppoſed ſcarcely
to have exceeded nine feet.   A conjecture formed
from the lower part of the Towers at the Weſt end

EDWARD IV (who ſucceeded the Founder) of the
houſe of York, was naturally no zealous promoter
of the laudable intentions of his predeceſſor as he
deprived the College of many lands and revenues,*
which

" ſame injudicious kind, in that compliment which he pays
" to Homer in the following verſes

cujuſque ex ore profuſos

Omnis poſteritas latices in carmina duxit

(which is as much as if he had ſaid in plain Engliſh, *All
poſter have lapp'd up the ſtreams pouring down from his
mouth, it ſere for their poets,*)

" I could never read theſe lines without calling to mind
" thoſe grotefque heads, which are fixed to the roof of the old
" Building of KING s College in Cambridge, which the in-
" genious architect has repreſented in the act of vomiting out
" the rain that falls thro' certain pipes moſt judiciouſly ſtuck
" in their mouths for that purpoſe Mr Addiſon recom-
" mends a method of trying the propriety of a metaphor, by
" drawing it out in viſible repreſentation Accordingly, I
" think this curious conceit of the builder might be em-
" ployed to the advantage of the youth in that Univerſity,
" and ſerve for as proper an illuſtration of the abſurdity of
" the poet's image, as that ancient picture which Ælian
" mentions, where Homer was figured with a ſtream running
" from his mouth, and a groupe of poets lapping it up at a
' diſtance "—For this note, and the tranſlation of ſome Latin epitaphs, which hereafter occur, I am indebted to a friend

* ' He took away a thouſand pounds a year in land, a-
' mong which was the fee-farm of the manors of Cheſterton
' and Cambridge Whereupon no fewer than forty of the
' Fellows and Scholars, befides Conducts, Clerks, Choriſters,
' and

which he gave to the Oxonians who were about his court. Nor was the Building much advanced in the short and turbulent reigns of Edward V and Richard III but Henry VII. in whom the line of Lancaster was restored, began, in the latter end of his reign, to complete the work of the Founder, expending 2000l. and presenting the College with the sum of 5000l for the purpose of finishing the Chapel Nor yet content with these singular marks of favour towards his pious predecessor, he even proposed it to Pope Alexander VI. and also to Pope Julius II. to canonise HENRY VI. which, however, by the extreme avarice of these Pontiffs, who would have granted that honour to the Prince's gold, ‡ and not his sanctity, was never effected.

' and other College-Officers, were in one day forced to de-
' part the House, for want of maintenance Indeed I have read
' that King Edward afterwards restored 500 marks of yearly
' revenue, on condition they should acknowledge him for
' their Founder, and write all their deeds in his name ;
' which perchance, for the present, they were contented to
' perform However his restitution was nothing adequate to
' the injury offered the Foundation, insomuch that Leland
' complains *Grantam suam hanc jacturam semper sensuram*, that
' his Cambridge for ever will be sensible of this loss '
                        Fuller's Church-History.

‡ The following account of what the Pope esteemed requisites for HENRY's canonization I shall produce, for the reader's entertainment, from Fuller, whose simplicity of style may not, perhaps, be unpleasing to many.
  " The King *(Henry VII)* had a moneth's minde (keep-
" ing seven years in that humour) to procure the Pope to
" canonize King HENRY the Sixth for a Saint For Eng-
" lish Saints, so frequent before the Conquest, were grown
" great dainties since that time France lately had her
" Saint Lewis, and why should not England receive the like
" favour, being no less beneficial to the Church of Rome?
" Nor could the unhappiness of our King HENRY (because
" deposed from his throne) be any just bar to his Saintship,
" seeing generally God's best servants are most subject to the
                        " sharpest

fected. Laftly, he ordered at his deceafe, that his
executors fhould fuppl᷑ the College, from time to
time, with different fums of money fufficient for completing the Building.

T***H***IS

" fharpeft afflictions. His canonizing would add much
" luftre to the line of Lancafter, which made his kinfman
" and mediate fucceffor King Henry the Seventh fo defirous
" thereof. Befides, well might he be made a Saint, who
" had been a Prophet For when the wars between Lanca-
" fter and Y*ork* firft began, H*enry* the Sixth beholding
" this Henry the Seventh, then but a boy playing in the
" Court, faid to the ftanders-by, ' See this youth will one
' day quietly enjoy what we at this time fo much fight about '
" This made the King with much importunity to tender this
" his requeft unto the Pope. A requeft the more reafona-
" ble, becaufe it was well nigh fourty years fince the death
" of that H*enry*, fo that only the fkeletons of his virtues
" remained in mens memories, the flefh and corruption (as
" one may fay) of his faults being quite confumed and for-
" gotten.

" Pope Alexander the Sixth, inftead of granting his re-
" queft, acquainted him with the requifites belonging to the
" making of a Saint Firft, that to confer that honour (the
" greateft on earth) was only in the power of the Pope, the
" proper judg of mens merits therein.   Secondly, that
" Saints were not to be multiplied but on juft motions, left
" commonnefs fhould caufe their contempt.   Thirdly, that
" his life muft be exemplarily holy, by the teftimony of cre-
" dible witneffes.   Fourthly, that fuch muft atteft the truth
" of real miracles wrought by him after death Fifthly, that
" very great was the *coft* thereof, becaufe all Chaunters,
" Chorifters, Bell-ringers, (not the leaft clapper in the ftee-
" ple wagging except money was tied to the end of the
" rope) with all the Officers of the Church of Saint Peter,
" together with the Commiffaries and Notaries of the Court,
" with all the Officers of the Pope's Bed-chamber, to the
" very Lock-fmiths, ought to have their feveral fees of fuch
" canonization.   Adding, that the total fumme would a-
" mount to fifteen hundred duckets of gold.

" *Tantæ molis erat Romanum condere Sanctum.*
" So vaft the work to form a Roman faint.

" Concluding

THIS is the only account (imperfect as it is) of the progress of the Edifice, which I could have offered to the Public, had not a Reverend Gentleman to whom

" Concluding with that which made the charges, though
" not *infinite*, *indefinite*, that the costs were to be multi-
" plied, SECUNDUM CANONIZATI POTENTIAM, according
" to the power and dignity of the person to be canonized.
" And certain it was, that the court of Rome would not
" behold this HENRY the Sixth in the notion which he died
" in, as a poor prisoner, but as he lived a King, so long as
" he had this Henry his kinsman to pay for the same.

" Most of these requisites met in King HENRY the Sixth
" in a competent measure First, the holiness of his life was
" confessed by all, save that some sullen persons suggested
" that his simplicity was above his sanctity, and his life
" pious, not so much out of hatred, as ignorance of badness.
" As for Miracles, there was no want of them, if credible
" persons might be believed : two of whose miracles it will
" not be amiss to recite

" Thomas Fuller, a very honest man, living at Ham-
" mersmith, near London, had a hard hap accidentally to
" light into the company of one who had stolen and driven
" away cattle; with whom, though wholly innocent, he
" was taken, arraigned, condemned, and executed. When
" on the gallows, Blessed King HENRY (loving justice
" when alive, and willing to preserve innocence, after death)
" appeared unto him, so ordering the matter, that the halter
" did not strangle him. For having hung an whole hour,
" and being taken down to be buried, he was found alive :
" for which favour he repaired to the tomb of King HENRY
" at Chertsey, (as he was bound to do no less) and there pre-
" sented his humble and hearty thanks unto him for his de-
" liverance. The very same accident, *mutatis mutandis*,
" varying only in the difference of place and persons, (with
" some addition about the Virgin Mary) hapned to Richard
" Boyes, dwelling within a mile of Bath, the story so like,
" all may believe them equally true.

" All the premisses required to a Saint appearing in
" some moderate proportion in HENRY the Sixth, especially
" if charitably interpreted, (Saints themselves need some fa-
" vour to be afforded them) it was the general expectation,

C   " that

whom my moſt grateful thanks on this occaſion are
due) been pleaſed to communicate to me the following
particulars.

" For carrying on this (*the Chapel*) and other
" buildings of the College, the Founder ſettled *per*
" *Annum* 'till the whole work ſhould be completed,
" a part of his Dutchy of Lancaſter, which for that
" purpoſe he veſted in feoffees.

" On the 4th of March, 1446, (A R 25) he granted
" to the Provoſt and Scholars for ever a quarry of
" ſtone, called Theſdale-quarry, in the lordſhip of
" Heſelwode, in the county of York. a perpetual
" grant of which he obtained of the Lord of the
                                        " Manor

" that he ſhould be ſuddenly canonized. But Pope Alexan-
" der the Sixth delaied, and in effect denied King Henry's
" deſire herein; yea, Julius his next ſucceſſor of continuance
" (not to mention the ſhort-liv'd Pius the Third) continued
" as ſturdy in his denial

" Men variouſly conjecture why the Pope in effect ſhould
" deny to canonize Henry the Sixth   a witty, but tart rea
" ſon is rendered by a noble Pen *(Lord Bacon)* becauſe the
" Pope would put a difference betwixt a *Saint* and an *Inno-*
" *cent*   But others conceive King Henry not ſo ſimple
" himſelf, his parts only ſeeming the lower, being over-
" topped with a high-ſpirited Queen   more probable it is
" what another ſaith, that ſeeing King Henry held the
" Crown by a falſe title, from the true heir thereof, the
" Pope could not, with ſo good credit, faſten a Saintſhip to
" his memory. But our great Antiquary reſolveth all in the
" Pope's covetouſneſs, *In cauſâ fuit Pontificis avaritia*, de-
" manding more than thrifty King Henry the Seventh would
" allow; who at laſt contented himſelf (by the Pope's leave
" hardly obtained) to remove his corps from Chertſey in
" Surrey, where it was obſcurely interred, to Windſor Cha
" pel, a place of greater reputation   Thus is he whom au-
" thors have obſerved *twice* crowned, *twice* depoſed, *twice*
" buried. The beſt was, though he was not canonized, yet
" there was plenty of Popiſh Saints beſide him, wherewith
" the Calendar is ſo overſtocked, that for want of room they
" juſtle one another."

" Manor (Henry Vanafour) with a way to carry the
" ftone through his lands directly to the river Querf
" (now Wharfe)

" On the 25th of February, 1448, he granted to
" the Provoft and Scholars of King's College, and
" the Provoft of Eton College, another quarry at
" Huddleftone near Shirborn, in Elmet, (not far from
" the former quarry) in the county of York, which
" he obtained a grant of from Sir John Langton and
" his fon It is probable, that the white ftone,
" which is feen about the Chapel, came from thefe
" quarries, the Yorkfhire ftone being generally of
" that colour How far the Building was raifed in the
" Founder's time is not certain, but it is probable
" that it was raifed pretty high at the Eaft end, and
" carried on floping towards the Weft, to the height
" of the white ftone

" Edward IV being proclaimed King (1460) an
" intire ftop was put to the works, for the Dutchy
" of Lancafter and the whole revenue of the Col-
" lege was feized by him part of which was re-
" granted to the Provoft and Scholars for their main-
" tenance, but nothing from the Dutchy for the
" Building

" In this manner was the work interrupted 'till
" about the nineteenth year of Edward IV. at which
" time Dr. Field, Warden of Winchefter College,
" and chaplain to Edward IV was chofen Provoft:
" who, by his intereft with the King and Dutchefs of
" York, feems to have promoted the Building. On
" the 10th of June 1479, he was appointed *Over-
                                                " feer

* It was not an uncommon thing formerly to appoint
fome Dignitary to prefide over the King's works Thus
William of Wickham (famous for his fkill in architecture)
was Overfeer of the works of Windfor Caftle, and Nicholas Clofe, Bifhop of Litchfield, was one, in whom Henry
VI placed fuch confidence, that he made him Overfeer and
Manager of all his intended Buildings for King's College.

He,

" feer of the works by the King, and continued 'till
" June 14, 14'3. During which time 1296l. 1s 8d.
" was expended on the works. of which 1000l. was
" given by the King, and 140l. by Thomas de Ro-
" therham, Bishop of Lincoln. and Chancellor of
" England. He was once a Fellow of the College.

" FROM the 14th of June, 1483, to the 22d of
" March following, nothing was done: at which
" time Thomas Cliff was by Richard III. appointed
" Overseer of the works, and continued so 'till the
" 23d of December following (1484) during which
" time 746l. 10s. 9d. was expended on the works: of
" which the King seems to have given 700l.

" AT this time the Eastern part of the Chapel ap-
" pears to have been carried up to the end of the East
" window (if not higher) and the two first Vestries
" towards the East on the North side, were covered
" in; but the Battlements were not yet set up. And
" thus

He, as I believe, (though some say his father) was Architect
of the Chapel; a work sufficient to distinguish his name
among the most shining characters of antiquity   John Can-
terbury, a native of Tewksbury, was Clerk of the works,
probably under the Bishop, and Fellow of the College in
1451. In the Indentures likewise we find the Arch-Deacon
of Norwich Overseer of the glass-work for the windows —
All knowledge of the Arts and Sciences centered, at that
time, in the Clergy.

Since I have now been mentioning persons employed in
this celebrated Building, I shall take the opportunity of adding also the names of two artists, who bore a share in the
work   These are preserved in the archives of Caius-College
in the following words.

" To alle Christen people this present writyng endented
" seeng, redyng, or heryng, John Wulrich Maistr Mason of
" the werks of the Kynges College Roial of our Lady and
" seynt Nicholas of Cambrigge, John Bell, Mason War-
" deyn in the fame werks, &c.   Written at Cambr. 17 Aug.
" 1476. 16 Edw. IV."

" thus the Building ftood floping towards the Weft
" end, † 'till May 28, 1508, (A. R. 23 Henry VII.)
" from which time the work went on at the expence
" of

† Some fuppofe that the Chapel was carried much higher
before this time, or, otherwife, fay they, it was almoft impof-
fible that Henry VII. fhould have finifhed the outer cafe of
ftone in the latter end of his reign, and even within the laft
year of it   But, in anfwer to this, it was not finifhed 'till
full feven years after his death —I fhall here, however, fet
down fome few particulars, from whence conjectures may be
drawn concerning the progrefs of the Building
   Within the long entry (above the Choir) on the North fide
of the ftone-roof, and on the outer wall, may be perceived
Toothings, where the Building was formerly joined
   Nearly in a line with thefe Toothings between the two
roofs, runs a principal beam; on which one may (by the
affiftance of candle-light) difcover the remains of mofs,
which once fpread about that part of it, which faces the Weft.
This fide of the beam bears a very different appearance from
all the others about the roof for it looks as if it had been a
long time expofed to the weather.   This is the fifteenth beam
from the Weft end.
   From thefe marks it is evident that the Building was not
raifed at once, but carried on by degrees, and not without
long and repeated intervals.   Even the plan of the work was
in fome few refpects changed.
   In the Veftries, on the South fide, the ftone door-cafes towards the Eaft differ in fhape from thofe that are nearer to
the Weft   Nor on the North fide, are the door-cafes, doors,
or roofs of the Veftries exactly uniform.   .
   The Buttreffes (which are twenty-two in number, eleven on
each fide of the Building) are not in every particular alike.
Five on the North fide, and four on the South fide of the Chapel are ornamented with crowns, rofes, portcullifes, griffins,
and other figures.   The remaining Buttreffes are plain and
unadorned
   Reflecting on thefe obfervations I am apt to imagine, that
Henry VII. when he took the work in hand, found a part of
the Building covered in with timber. (but I do not fay over-
laid with lead, as at prefent) that this timber-roof was then
                                                        extended

" of Henry VII and his executors, 'till the cafe of
" the Chapel was finifhed, on July 29, 1515: (A. R.
" 7th of Henry VIII) during which time the charges
" amounted to 11581l. 1s 1od of which in the firft
" year, viz from May 28, 1508, to April 1, 1509,
                                                        " was

extended over the Eaftern part of the Chapel , and continued
to that beam, which feems to have been once expofed to the
weather   And I farther fuppofe, that from the Toothings
(which are almoft in a level line with the beam)to the ornamented Buttreffes, the Walls and Buttreffes were raifed to a
great height, when Henry VII began to build   that this
Prince erected the remaining part of the Walls Weftward,
with the Bu treffes almoft from the ground   and, therefore,
fet up on the latter, as he carried on the work, the figures that
are feen at this day   Had he built any other Buttreffes, he
would, I fhould think, have ornamented them in the fame
manner

On the whole then my conclufion is, that that part of the
Building raifed with white ftone was erected by HENRY VI.
that the Eaftern half (or nearly half) of the Chapel was
roofed, and the Walls further carried on, at the joint expence of Edward IV. (who, notwithftanding his oppreffive
treatment of the fociety, prefented them with a fum of money
for this purpofe) Richard III Thomas de Rotherham, and
perhaps the College, who might have contributed it's fhare
towards the advancement of the Building —and that Henry
VII. finifhed, or rather left a legacy for finifhing, the outer
Walls and Buttreffes

A reader, who is no ftranger to the character of Henry
VII may well be furprized at any inftance of his liberality
But let it be remembered, that he did not begin to lay open
his treafures before the decline of his life, when he was
feized with horror and remorfe for the iniquities and feveri-
ties of his reign   An elegant Hiftorian expreffes himfelf, on
this occafion, in the following manner

   " To allay the terrors, under which he laboured, he en-
" deavoured by diftributing alms and founding religious,
" houfes, to make atonement for his crimes, and to purchafe
" by the facrifice of part of his ill-gotten treafures, a re
" conciliation with his offended Maker."

" was remitted from time to time to Dr. Hutton, Pro-
" voft of the College, the fum of 1408l. 12s 6d.

" On the firft day of March, 1500, Henry VII. by
" Indenture between him, and the Provoft and Scho-
" lars, gave 5000l for carrying on the Building, and
" bound himfelf and his executors to furnifh the Col-
" lege with further fums of money, 'till the Chapel
" fhould be completed : the Provoft and Scholars co-
" venanting on their part to lay out the money faith-
" fully, under the direction of fuch Overfeers as
" fhould be appointed by the King or his executors;
" and to give a true account how the faid money was
" expended, as often as they fhould be called there-
" unto by him or his executors   On the 8th of Fe-
" bruary, (A R 7th Henry VIII) the executors of
" Henry VII by Indentures between them and the
" Provoft and Scholars, gave 5000l. more —' to the
' intent that they (the Provoft and Scholars) and their
' fucceffors, by the advice, overfight and controlment
' of the faid executors or their deputies, fhall, as
' haftily as they may or can reafonably, without de-
' lay, vault the Church of the faid College, after the
' form of a plat therefore devifed and fubfcribed with
' the hand of the faid executors; and caufe double
' desks to be made in the choir of the faid Church,
' glaze all the Windows in the fame, with fuch ima-
' ges, ftories, arms, badges, and other devices, as fhall
' be devifed by the faid executors : and alfo clearly
' and wholly finifh, perform and end all the work
' that is not yet done in the faid Church, in all things
' within as well as without '

THE College neglected not this opportunity of completing their Chapel. For in the fame year,* (1513)
in which a fupply of money was granted, the Society
began to add a fecond and inner roof of ftone, in the
form of a grand Gothic arch, without fo much as the
appearance of a pillar to uphold it, the Buttreffes and
Towers

* See Indenture the firft.

Towers of the Chapel being it's only support. In the middle of this roof, and in the flatteſt part of it, are fixed perpendicularly, at equal diſtances from one another, ſtones, (adorned with roſes and portculliſes) every one of which is no leſs than a ton weight. Each of theſe is upwards of a yard * in thickneſs, and projects beyond the other parts of the carved work. The diſpoſition of the materials in this roof, and particularly of the ſtones abovementioned, (which were the wonder and the admiration of Sir Chriſtopher Wren † himſelf, one of the moſt celebrated architects who ever lived) may well be conſidered among the moſt remarkable curioſities of the Building; ſince there are many, and theſe no incompetent judges, who do not ſcruple to aſſert, that it would far exceed the skill of the architects of our preſent age to lay a roof of ſtone in the ſame form and order.

FULLER is more liberal of his praiſes on this roof, than on any other part of the Chapel.

    "THE Chapel in this College is one of the rareſt
"fabricks in Chriſtendom, wherein the ſtone-work,
"wood-work, and glaſs-work contend, which moſt
"deſerve admiration. Yet the firſt generally car-
"rieth away the credit, (as being a *Stone henge* in-
"deed) ſo geometrically contrived, that voluminous
"ſtones mutually ſupport themſelves in the arched
"roof, as if art had made them to forget nature, and
"weaned them from their fondneſs to deſcend to their
                                           "center.

---

* Though the thickneſs of theſe ſtones is exceeding great, yet the whole roof is not proportionably thick, being in ſome parts (between the ribs) not more than two inches thick

    Fuller ſomewhere ſays, though falſly, that the roof of the Chapel of St Mary, adjoining to the Cathedral of Ely, was the pattern from whence this roof was taken.

    † "There is a tradition that Sir Chriſtopher Wren went "once a year to ſurvey the roof of the Chapel of KING's "College, and ſaid, that if any man would ſhew him where to "place the firſt ſtone, he would engage to build ſuch ano- "ther."   Walpole's Anec. on Painting, vol 1, p 115.

" center And yet, though there be fo much of
" *Minerva*, there is nothing of *Arachne* in this
" Building I mean not a fpider appearing, or cob-
" web to be feen on the (Irifh wood or cedar) beams
" thereof No wonder then if this Chapel, fo rare
" a ftructure, was the work of three fucceeding
" Kings, HENRY the Sixth, who founded it, the
" Seventh, who farthered, the Eighth, who fi-
" nifhed it "

THE unlimited legacy of Henry VII was not
idly employed for in the 18th year of Henry VIII.
(1527) the beautiful Windows* of painted glafs were
fet up, which alone are fufficient to ennoble the age
that gave birth to the painters —But of the Windows
largely hereafter

EVERY part of the work about the Building, was
now haftening to a conclufion The Veftries,† which
are eighteen in number, nine on each fide of the Chapel) had been long fince covered in, and one, if not
more, of them already *endowed* For it is a well-
known

---

* It has been fuppofed, by perfons who have obferved the
arms of Henry VIII painted on the Windows, and the ini-
tial letter of his name, that they were glazed at his expence.
But the contrary conjecture bears a greater appearance of
probability, if we confider, that the difpofition of that Prince
was rapacious, and not liberal —We may, therefore, very
reafonably conclude, that after the death of Henry VII his
legacy was employed in finifhing the Building I muft, however, remark that a Bifhop of Norwich is faid to have contributed, though not voluntarily, towards glazing the Windows
The ftory related about him is this

" Robert Nix Bifhop of Norwich, having incurred a *Pre-*
" *munire* for extending his jurifdiction over the Mayor of
" Thetford, was fined for it with part of which fine, 'tis
" faid, the beautiful Windows of painted glafs in KING's
" College-Chapel, were purchafed "

Blomefield's Hiftory of Norfolk.

† The Plate of the Chapel will give the reader an idea of
the fituation of thefe Veftries

D

known circumstance, that these Vestries were formerly
called *Clantries* that they were employed in the ceremony of singing or saying Mass for the souls of
the deceased and that any Superiour of the society,
who was inclined to have that service performed for
his soul after death, endowed one of these Vestries for
that purpose

It appears from the Founder's Will quoted above,
that Altars would have been erected in all the Vestries,
had not the laws of the Reformation, which followed
some few years after the finishing of the Chapel, abo-
lished all superstitious rites belonging to the ancient
religion among which may very justly be numbered
the ceremony of singing Mass for departed souls

Certain it is, that much work was done to
wards erecting an Altar in the first Vestry, on the
North side, towards the West. In it are yet remaining, on a pavement raised above the other part of the
floor, two stone pillars very finely carved; which
originally belonged to an Altar In the second Vestry towards the West, on the South side, a part of the
wall, having many holes and pegs in it, is prepared for
the addition of some sort of ornament, which (if one
may be allowed to determine the intention from these
appearances) would have been somewhat of the same
kind, when completed, with the pillars above-men
tioned

Four of the Vestries have each a seat and a desk in
them, built for some Superiour, (perhaps the Provost
or Vice-Provost) whose duty it might be, or, more
probably, whose inclination might lead him to attend
the service of Mass The Priest, who officiated, always stood during the whole ceremony

The

‡ The service of Mass was nearly the same with the present Communion-service, excepting only a few additional
prayers about the souls of deceased persons The officiating
Priest received the Sacrament every day, but they, who attended, did not

THE moſt ancient of the little Chapels or Veſtries are the firſt* and ſecond* from the Eaſt, North ſide. The latter of theſe was the Chantry of William Towne, who lies buried in it, with a large, grey, marble ſlab over his grave on which is his figure formed in braſs at full length, in his doctoral robes, (ſuch as are worn at this day in the Univerſity) and ermine hood and bonnet, with a ſlit in his ſcarlet gown, (for ſuch an one is repreſented) from whence his hands are extended.—On his hands hangs a ſcrole with this diſtich

Gloria, fama ſcolis, laus, artes, cetera mundi
   Vana nimis valeant ſpes mea ſola Deus.

Farewell to glory, to reputation in learning, to praiſe, to the arts, to all the vanity of this world. God is my only hope.

Under his feet is the following inſcription:

Orate pro anima Magiſtri Willi Towne, Doctoris in Theologia, quondam ſocii hujus Collegii, qui obiit XI° die menſis Marcii, anno Incarnationis Dominice M° CCCC° LXXXXIV° Cujus animæ propitietur Deus Amen.

THE words *Orate pro anima*, and *Cujus animæ propitietur Deus*, are effaced †

PRAY FOR THE SOUL OF Maſter ‡ William Towne, Doctor

---

* Theſe Veſtries only were built, when Dr Towne died. —The fret-work of the roofs of theſe differ ſomewhat from the reſt

† The zeal of the Reformers, in 1645, was much offended at any inſcription which began and ended with words like theſe Hence we find many tomb-ſtones robbed of this part of their epitaphs—KING's Chapel fortunately ſuſtained no conſiderable injury from the fury of fanaticks, though examples of ruin and deſolation, in buildings ornamented like itſelf, were, in the preceding century, to be lamented in almoſt every quarter

‡ The dignity of *Cuſtos* (or Maſter) of King's Hall was offered to him but I cannot ſay whether he accepted it or

Doctor of Divinity, once a Fellow * of this College, who died on the eleventh day of March, 1494 Whose soul God pardon Amen

In this Veftry, no doubt Mafs was faid many years for Dr Towne For he left a yearly revenue of four marks† for fome ore of the Fellows, who fhould be a Prieft, to fay Mafs and fing Dirges for delivering his foul from purgatory —The Altar ftood with in the Eaftern angle ——Within this Veftry there is a fire-place ‡

The moft ancient, after Dr Towne's is the Chantry of Dr Argentine which is the Veftry on the South fide, neareft to the Eaft His figure is placed, according to his laft defire, on the tombftone, in his doctoral robes, with his hands elevated towards the upper part of the ftone, where there was formerly placed a crucifix From his mouth proceed thefe words

Virginis atque Dei fili, crucifixe, Redemptor
Humani generis, Chrifte memento mei

O

not —King's Hall was a College (ftanding on part of the ground where Trinity College is now built) formerly very refpectable for the learning of it's Members This was united with two other Hoftels into one magnificent College, (now called Trinity College) by Henry VIII

* Dr Towne was one of the twelve Scholars placed in the College by HENRY VI at it's firft inftitution in 1441

† A mark is eight ounces of filver Valuing then each ounce at five fhillings, the yearly revenue, with which Dr Towne endowed his Chantry, amounts to eight pounds This will appear no inconfiderable fum, if we confider the fcarcity of money in former ages

‡ In Roman Catholic churches we find fire-places ufed for burning incenfe, and other religious fervices The fire place in Dr Towne's Chantry was built for fimilar purpofes.—It may be obferved, that there is a door in this Veftry leading to the high Altar where the charcoal taken from the fire-place, and depofited in an incenfe box, was carried at the celebration of Mafs.

O Chrift, fon of God and the Virgin, crucified Lord, Redeemer of mankind, remember me

THE crucifix is torn away, I fuppofe, by fome fanatic reformer.

Under his feet is the following infcription :

Artifte, Medici, Scripture interpretis alme,
Argentem corpus fepelit lapis ifte Johannis.
Qui tranfis, recolas, morieris cernuus ora
Spiritus in Chrifto vivat i unquam moriturus.

THIS ftone buries the body of John Argentem, Mafter of Arts, Phyfician, Preacher of the Gofpel. Paffenger, remember thou art mortal pray in an humble pofture, that my foul may live in Chrift, in a ftate of immortality

ON labels which run round the tombftone thefe words are engraved

Orate pro anima Johannis Argentem, Artium Magiftri, Medicinarum Doctoris, alme Scripture Profefforis, et hujus Collegii prepofiti, qui obiit Anno Domini millefimo, quingentefimo feptimo, et die menfis Februarii fecundo Cujus anime propitietur Deus Amen.

PRAY FOR THE SOUL OF John Argentem, Mafter of Arts, Doctor of Phyfic and Divinity, and Provoft of this College, who died Feb 2, 1507 For whofe foul may God be atoned. Amen

WITHIN this Veftry is a pavement, raifed above the furface of the floor, for an Altar

THE Veftry which was next confecrated to religious ufes, for the foul of Robert Hacomblen, is the fecond from the Weft, South fide The effigies of the deceafed lies dreffed in doctoral robes, as well as the former of whom I have fpoken On a label proceeding from his mouth is infcribed the following line,

Vulnera, Chrifte, tua mihi dulcis fit me licina

O Chrift, be thy wounds my pleafing remedy.

ON the brazen labels, which on all fides furround the ftone, are thefe words.

Domine, fecundum actum meum noli me judicare.
Nihil dignum in confpectu tuo egi

Ideo

Ideo deprecor majeſtatem tuam,
Ut tu, Deus, deleas iniquitatem meam.
Jeſu, miſerere.

O Lord, judge me not according to my actions
I have done nothing worthy in thy ſight
Therefore I beſeech thy majeſty;
That thou, O God, wouldeſt blot out mine iniquity
    Have mercy, Jeſu

THE inſcription that was under his feet, is taken away; probably on account of the words *Orate pro anima*, and *Cujus animæ propitietur Deus*

ON each corner of the braſs labels running around the tomb-ſtone are figures emblematical of the four Evangeliſts, with their names in Gothic letters

THIS Chantry of Dr Hacomblen,* who was Provoſt when the Windows were ſet up, is more beautifully ornamented than any of the others   The centre of the roof is gilded, and towards the middle of the South window are two exceeding fine portraits that to the left being a lively repreſentation of the Founder, the other of St Nicholas   In the ſmall compartments (or *Crockets* as they are commonly called) of the upper part of the window, are the figures of Biſhops on the left, and of ſome animals on the right.   In the higheſt crocket (which is exactly in the middle of the window) and in the upper part of the crocket, are painted the arms of Henry VIII.   Underneath theſe is a cipher (I believe) of Hacomblen's name.   On the left of the cipher is a red Roſe · on the right a mixture of the red and white Roſes, denoting the Union of the two Houſes of York and Lancaſter. Below the cipher are the Arms of the College, viz. Sable, † three Roſes Argent. † Party, firſt Azure, a
                        Flower-

---

* Dr Hacomblen, overſeeing the works, had a great opportunity of adorning this Chantry for himſelf

† The perpetuity of the College is ſignified by the unchangeableneſs of the Black it's fruitfulneſs in producing the moſt beautiful flowers in literature by the three Roſes Argent:

Flower-de-Luce, * and next Gules, a Lion* Paffant,
Or The Arms, as well as the Rofes in this crocket,
make a very elegant appearance. Nor will the fpectator behold without a pleafing fatisfaction the Salutation of Mary, the figure of Chrift, &c. on the oppo-
lite window, that looks towards the Ante Chapel.——
On the fame window are feen the initials of Hacomblen's name.——I muft further obferve, that on the
Eaft lide of this Veftry is a picture of St Nicholas:
and, on the Weft fide, an human skull is well figured
in ftone.——The noble monument in this Veftry was
erected in honour of John Churchill, Marquis of
Blandford (fon of the great Duke of Marlborough)
who died in this College (1702) in the fixteenth year
of his age

THE only remaining Veftry, which I fuppofe to
have been employed as a Chantry, is the third from
the Weft, on the South fide This was endowed in
the days of Queen Mary, by Dr Braffie, when Popery, though well nigh extirpated in the preceding
reign, began once more to raife it's head within this
ifland.

On the outfide of the door, and underneath the
two upper pannels, are fome fmall remains of an infcription, that was once covered with horn. An entire part of the horn and parchment (on which the
words were written) is yet to be perceived under the
panel towards the right The infcription (in compliance with Dr Braffie's defire) formerly contained
thefe words,

*Orate pro anima Roberti Braffie, quondam prepofiti
hujus Collegis.*

PRAY FOR THE SOUL of Robert Braffie, formerly
Provoft of this College.

ON

On a label proceeding from his mouth was once engraved,

Deus propitius esto mihi peccatori
God be merciful to me a sinner.
Under his feet we may read these words

Hic jacet Robertus Brassie, sacre Theologie Professor, quondam Prepositus hujus Collegii, qui ab hac vita decessit decimo die Novembris, Anno Domini M° CCCCC° LVIII°

HERE lies Robert Brassie, Doctor of Divinity, formerly Provost of this College, who departed this life November 10, A. D. 1558 *

On the window which is next to the Ante-Chapel his name is painted —In this Vestry likewise a pavement is raised for an Altar.

THESE

---

* The deceased, of whose epitaphs I have been speaking, are all buried in the Vestries about the Chapel.—What use was really made of the cemetery or church-yard, consecrated by the Bishops of Salisbury and Lincoln (see page 13) three years before the foundation of the Chapel, I cannot venture to say. It was intended, however, at the consecration, as a burying-ground for the Rector and twelve Scholars, who were the first Members of the College, and it was contained within that spot lying next to the river, and opposite to the West end of Chapel, which is now converted into a bowling-green and garden. When the plan of the Chapel was formed, it was designed that a square cloister should have been continued from the West door of the Chapel to the cemetery or burying-ground, and in the middle of the West side of the cloister a stone tower for a ring of bells. With these latter the College was provided, and as neither the cloister nor tower were ever finished, they were hung within a wooden tower erected for that purpose at about the distance of thirty yards from the West door. But the tower decaying (and the bells becoming useless) it was taken down some few years ago, and the materials were removed.—Some remains of the foundation of the wooden tower are yet to be seen.

But I shall here present my reader with a plan not only of the cloister, of which I have been treating, but also of the intended College, (described page 12) with which I am favoured

THESE four Veſtries, of which I have treated, were once (I do not ſcruple to ſay) made uſe of for Maſs-Service

by a Gentleman, whoſe reputation for ſkill in architecture is too well known and eſtabliſhed to receive an addition from any humble conmendations that I might be able to beſtow

a is the preſent Chapel forming the North ſide of the intended Square b the Eaſt ſide of the ſame in the middle of which

a gate would have been hung opening towards Trumpington-ſtreet, (ſee page 12.) c the South ſide of the Square which would have contained a part of the Provoſt's lodging d, and ſeveral chambers — e the Weſt ſide of the Square . which would have contained a Lecture-Room at f , and a Hall at g , and, in the middle of this ſide (e) an opening would have led thro' a long paſſage h, towards the bridge. K the kitchen-Court which would have conſiſted of a Kitchen, Brewhouſe, Bakehouſe, and other offices the South ſide l belonging to the Provoſt , the Weſt ſide m, and the North ſide n to the College N would have been the large court formed by the four ſides a, b, c, e and p a Conduit in the middle of the ſame q the Weſt door of the Chapel a ;

from

Service said or sung for the souls of departed men *

THERE is yet another inscription, and that of such exalted sentiments, that it would reflect an honour on the memory of the greatest and wisest men. This epitaph, which may be found within the sixth Vestry from the East, North side, is conceived in the following simple and modest expressions

Aperiet Deus tumulos, et educet
Nos de sepulcris.
Qualis eram, dies isthæc cum
Venerit, scies
Terræ creditus, die 30mo Augusti,
Annoque a nato Domino 1679.

God will lay open the graves, and bring forth
All men from their sepulcres
It will be known, when that day
Shall come, what manner of man I was.
Buried the 30th of August, 1679.

ABOVE the inscription is his Coat of Arms.

THIS person's name was Thomas Crouch He bequeathed several hundred volumes to the College Library.

I

from whence the passage r leads to the square cloister s, t, v, u, ; whereof t and v, the North and South sides, would have contained severally in length 200 feet s and w, the East and West sides, each 175 feet X the burying-ground (mentioned page 13) lying within the four sides of the Cloister w the inward door (for outward there would have been none) leading into the Tower y, intended for a ring of Bells This Tower, therefore, would have been erected at no great distance from the river

* The frequent mention made of Mass has reminded me of Holy-Water This (for it is usually placed either in a niche close to the Church door without, or just within the Church) was probably set in one vase under the brazen monument on the South side, and in another next the North door, on the opposite side But this being nothing more than mere conjecture, is submitted to the judgment of the discerning reader —The niches on each side of the porches, and of the West-door, were intended for statues.

I am defired to add the following remark on the in-fcription above-mentioned.

The Spectator, in one of his papers, introduces an epitaph which bears the nearest refemblance to the above-mentioned infcription.—The following are the words.

Hic jacit R. C in expectatione diei fupremi. Qualis erat, dies ifte indicabit.

Here lieth R. C in expectation of the laft day. What fort of a man he was, that day will difcover.

On this epitaph the Spectator thus expreffes himfelf.

" The thought of it is ferious, and in my opi-
" nion the fineft that I ever met with upon this occa-
" fion. It is ufual, after having told us the name of
" the perfon who lies interred, to launch out into his
" praifes. This epitaph takes a quite contrary turn,
" having been made by the perfon himfelf fome time
" before his death "

See the Spectator, Vol VII No 518.

There are, indeed, many other infcriptions on the tomb-ftones in the Veftries: but thefe are all very le-gible, and contain nothing remarkable

The remaining Veftries (of which I have not al-ready treated) on the South fide, are now converted into a Library, (for the common ufe of the College) in which are fome thoufands of curious and valuable books

Among many choice manufcripts in the Library is the Book of Pfalms upon parchment, four fpans in length, and three in breadth which is faid to have been taken from the Spaniards at the fiege of Cadiz, (in Elizabeth's reign, 1591) and thence brought into England with other Spoils

I fhall now proceed to give the dimenfions of the Chapel on the Outfide

The length from Eaft to Weft contains - 316 feet.
The breadth from North to South - - 84 feet.
The height from the ground to the top of
    the Battlements - - - - - - - 90 feet.

The

The height from the ground to the top of
the Pinnacles is somewhat more than - 101 feet,
The height from the ground to the top of
any one of the Corner-Towers* - - 146½ feet
THE dimensions of the inside are as follows.
The length from East to West contains - 291 feet.
The breadth from North to South - - 45½ feet
The height - - - - - - 78 feet

THE walls on the inside of the Ante-Chapel † are
adorned with a variety of carved stone of exquisite
workmanship, scarcely to be equalled, representing the
Arms of the Houses of York and Lancaster , with
many Crowns, ‡ Roses, Portcullises, and Flower de-
Luces   What is peculiarly remarkable in this carv-
ing

---

* The workmanship of the Towers (which terminate in
domes) erected at the four corners of the Chapel, is extremely
noble, abounding with a variety of ornament   In each of
them are winding stairs leading to the two roofs of the Building —These Towers contribute greatly to cause that fine
effect, which a view of the Chapel on the outside produces on
the sight

† The Ante-Chapel will be paved in a most elegant man
ner

‡ The Crowns are emblematical of Royalty ; the Chapel
being built by *King's*

The white and red Roses were the devices of the two Houses
of York and Lancaster , and much regarded, as distinguishing
emblems of these parties, when the Chapel was built —This
suggests a reason, why figures of roses are every where dif-
persed about the building

The Portcullis was the Arms of the Tudor family , and
consequently of Henry VII who contributed towards finishing the Chapel

The Flower-de-Luce was brought over from France, after
the conquest of that kingdom by Henry V the father of the
Founder

Hence the reader may perceive, that the ornamental figures
of Crowns, &c. about the Chapel, were not chosen fantasti-
cally, and without reason

ing is, that of all the Crowns and Rofes, numerous as they are, there is not one, which, upon a clofe examination, will not be found, in fome refpect, differing from all the others

IN the middle of one of thefe Rofes (on the Weft fide, towards the South) may be feen a fmall figure of the Virgin Mary after which foreigners make frequent enquiries, and never fail to pay it a religious reverence, croffing their breafts at the fight, and addreffing it with a fhort prayer

ABOUT the middle of the Chapel there is a partition of wood curioufly carved, feparating the Ante-Chapel from the Choir This partition was built at the time when Anne Boleyn was Queen (1534) to Henry VIII On the front of it are many lover's knots, and in a panel neareft to the wall on the right are the Arms of Anne Boleyn impaled with thofe of her Royal Husband and in one of the panels, on the fame fide, is carved a moft lively reprefentation of the Almighty cafting down the rebellious Angels from Heaven This fmall piece of fculpture is univerfally admired

CONCERNING this I find the following words in *An Account of publick Buildings*, &c

" On the Organ loft is a fine piece of fculpture,
" being the figure of an old man, furrounded with
" Angels, and Hell torments under his feet; for which
" they tell you 6000l has been offered, though it
" be not three quarters of a yard in diameter."

I have quoted this paffage in order to fhew the notice of which this piece of fculpture is thought worthy. For as to the fum faid to have been offered for it, I do not fuppofe any one will credit it

ON the left of the choir door, and in the panel neareft to it, the fupporters of the Arms (of Henry VIII) are executed with a fkill that is fcarcely to be exceeded

ON the partition ftands a ftately Organ. which, however, does not prevent a full view of the beautiful Roof, from the great Weft door to the Eaft window

A

A view, fufficient to ftrike the mind of every common beholder with rapture and admiration

On the fame partition are fixed nine Colours, taken from the ifland of Manila by Sir William Draper (late Fellow of King's College) who commanded the British troops at the reduction of the city of Manila   The city and ifland were attacked and conquered in 1762 and the General (who was at that time a Member of the Society) at his return, by his Majefty's permiffion, prefented the College with thefe trophies of his victory.

Underneath the Organ, through folding doors finely carved, (on which are feen the Arms of James I. in whofe reign the doors were fet up) you enter the Choir, which is aftonifhingly grand   The Stalls, of which there are two rows on each fide of the Chapel, are of carved wood.   Both fides of the Choir were wainfcotted at the expence of Thomas Weaver, Fellow of the College in 1595.

The back part of the upper Stalls (appointed for graduate Fellows) is made up of thirty-four panels in fifteen of which, on each fide of the Choir, are carved the Arms of all the Kings of England from Henry V to James I   the Arms of the two Univerfities Cambridge and Oxford, and of the two Colleges King's and Eton.   The fupporters of thefe Arms advance out from the panels in full proportion, being made after life: and, indeed, the greateft part of the carved work about the Building is in *Alto Relievo*   On the right and left of a fpectator entering the Choir, are the Provoft's and Vice-Provoft's feats   At the back of the Provoft's ftall are carved St George and the Dragon, (with fome other figures) which deferve a particular notice; as the work of thefe is executed in an almoft inimitable manner

The lower row of ftalls contains nearly the fame number of feats with the upper immediately above it and it is appointed for the under-graduate Fellows, the Scholars, and the finging Clerks.   Under thefe lower

ftalls

ftalls are erected benches , on two of which fit the Chorifters on each fide of the Chapel

THERE is much work beftowed even on the feats of the ftalls ; all which may be raifed upwards or downwards by turning them on their hinges

IN the middle of the Choir ftands a brazen desk, at which are read the leffons appointed for the day On the top of it ftands the figure of HENRY VI. This was given by Dr Hacomblen, formerly (1509) a Provoft of the College , in whofe Provoftfhip the grand Roof and Windows were begun and finifhed.

THE pavement of the Choir is of black and white marble ; which, though it's beauty is much effaced by the dampnefs of the foil underneath, ftill preferves a rich and coftly appearance.

THE Altar-piece is decent, though not grand. But as a more noble one, and in every refpect anfwerable to the magnificence of the Chapel, will be erected, I fhall fay but little of the prefent You afcend it by four fteps On the table ftands an exceedingly curious filver difh : in the middle of which is reprefented the laft fupper of our Saviour. This was given by Sir Thomas Page, formerly (1675) a Provoft of the College Befides the difh there are two very large filver candlefticks, which make a noble appearance There is too a fmall filver difh belonging to the Altar wrought in a moft extraordinary manner.

HAVING now given a general view of the Chapel, as well as a particular defcription of moft things worthy of our notice, I fhall proceed to an explanation of the Windows With regard to the curiofity of which I fhall firft remark, that there is fcarcely found any thing of the kind equal to them in Europe The form of them is Gothic, like thofe Windows that are feen in old churches. On them are painted ftriking pieces, made up of the moft lively colours, reprefenting different parts of the Hiftory contained in the *Old* and *New* Teftament.

THE

The large Windows about the Chapel are in number twenty-six; besides many smaller belonging to the Veftries. The former are all painted with colours inconceivably beautiful, except the great Weft Window, which feems to have been left plain in order to give light to the Chapel, it admitting more light than one half of the others. But this is dubious, as the fifth Indenture (fee the end of the Book) contracts for the painting of this among fome other Windows.

I know it has been commonly faid, that all the Windows of the Chapel were once taken down and hidden through fear of Oliver Cromwell, left he (in compliance with the fanatick opinions he profeffed) fhould deftroy them as relicks of Popery, and that, through the confufion this occafioned, one of them (which it is pretended was the Weft Window) was either ftolen or loft. But no fuch accident ever happened. though there were undoubtedly Vifitors fent down by the *Long Parliament* to CAMBRIDGE, whofe bufinefs it was to remove every fuperftitious ornament about the Univerfity They indeed in purfuance of this commiffion, ordered the Organ * at that time in ufe to be taken down, and fold the pipes, but offered not the flighteft injury to the Windows fparing them moft probably at the interceffion of Dr. Whitchcot, then Provoft, who was promoted to that dignity by the *Long Parliament* The image, however, of the Virgin Mary (over the South door, within the Choir) did not efcape, as 'tis faid, the hands of fome furious enthufiaft, who, in a fit of religious frenzy, effaced an object fo offenfive to his fight

THAT the reader may the more eafily underftand the fituation of the paintings, I fhall firft premife, that each Window is feparated by what among architects
are

---

* The inner pipes of the prefent Organ were fet up in the reign of William and Mary. As to the outer cafe, it was never taken down.

are called Munions into five Lights. § These Lights are divided, about the middle, into an upper and lower part, by a Stone Transom. § In the upper parts are reprefented different pieces of History felected from the Old Teftament. Thofe in the lower relate entirely to the New.

Of the five Lights, (in all the Windows except the Eaftern) both in the upper and lower divifions, there is one, namely, *that Light which is in the Middle,* on which are defcribed figures of Saints * or Angels, (two in the upper parts and two in the lower) with labels affixed to each, explaining the Paintings on the Lights placed on either fide of them. (See the fecond Window, page 43.) On thefe Lights then (fituated to the right and left of the Saints and Angels are painted the Hiftorical pieces above-mentioned: of all which I fhall treat in their proper order. †

But before I begin my explanation, I muft beg the reader will obferve with peculiar attention the correfpondence between the Paintings of the fame
Window

§ The Plate of the Chapel will very well ferve to illuftrate thefe remarks

* Whether the figures in the middle Light reprefent Angels and Roman Saints, according to fome, or deceafed Popes, according to others ; or even the ancient Fathers of the Church, according to a ftill different opinion, is a queftion that I cannot determine nor is it a matter of any great importance They are, however, by many, and not improperly, termed Messengers , becaufe they deliver an account of the fubject of the paintings on either fide of them. The face of each Meffenger is generally turned towards that Painting, which the label around it explains —The countenances of many of them are finely executed, and well deferve a peculiar attention. They are chiefly as large as life —The particular beauties among thefe figures I leave to the notice of the fpectator, being ftudious of brevity.

† In the Crockets of all the Windows are painted figures of Crowns, Rofes, Flower-de-Luces, and Portcullifes , with the letters H K (Henry and Queen Katherine) H R. (Henricus Rex) In the higheft and middle Crocket are painted the Arms of Henry VIII

F

Window, in the upper and lower divisions. As fo
xample. In the upper division a piece of Histor)
taken from the Old Testament is painted on tw(
Lights on the left side of a Window. In the lowe
division, on the fame fide, on two Lights immediatel)
underneath those in the upper part, is painted fome
circumstance selected from the New Testament, cor
responding to that above it from the Old.

I have cited quotations from Scripture, and affixed
them to my explanation of every single piece · chiefl)
for the fake of describing more minutely the circum
stances of each Painting, (which, as a Spectator will
observe, is generally a perspective.) This method, I
hope, will be particularly approved by those, who
shall make use of my book while they are surveying
the Windows

THE lower divisions of the Windows on the North
side contain a part of our Saviour's History, including
some short time before his birth; the last of the Paintings describing the circumstance of his being scourged
before Pontius Pilate ——With the *second* Window
(towards the West) of this side I shall begin my
explanation. the design of the *first* being utterly
inexplicable.‡　　　　　　　　　　　　　　The

‡ The first Window from the West, North side, and the first
and second from the West, South side, differ both in beauty
and colour from the rest. These three I am unable to explain
through the confusion of the painting, (for part of the glafs
seems to have been put together without any order, scarcely a
figure being preserved entire) though I have employed dili-
gent pains and enquiries to effect it.——What unlucky accident
occasioned their present shatter'd condition, I cannot even
suppose but I shall offer the following conjecture about them.
It is certain, that painted glafs, very different from what is
now seen, was fixed up in the East Window, and in the Half
Window (South side) in the reign of Richard III and that
the same was taken down in the reign of Henry VIII in or
der to fit up the paintings that are placed in them at this day
——It is conjectured, that the three Windows, which seem inexplicable, were made chiefly out of the old glafs taken
from the two Windows abovementioned.

UPPER DIVISION.

Left Side.

These two Lights reprefent an offering which was prefented to God by Jofeph and Mary before their efpoufals *—What the offering is, I cannot determine If we fuppofe a *facrifice*, then this piece feems not only to allude to the painting about Jepthah underneath, but to be a kind of an introductory painting to the Hiftory of Chrift For Jewifh *farrifices* are faid to have forefhewn the *facrifice* of Chrift.

Right Side.

The efpoufals of Tobias and Sarah.

" Then he called his
" daughter Sarah, and fhe
" came to her father, and
" he took her by the hand,
" and gave her to be wife
" to Tobias."
Tobit, chap, xvii. ver 13.

An Angel.

A Saint.

LOWER DIVISION.

Jepthah offering his daughter.*

" And it came to pafs at
" the end of two months
" that fhe returned unto
" her father, who did with
" her according unto his
" vow which he had vowed"
Judges, chap. iii. ver. 39.

* Thefe two Paintings are, as I am apt to believe, mifplaced. If the Painting of Jepthah offering be removed into the upper divi-

The efpoufals of Jofeph and Mary

" Then Jofeph being
" raifed from fleep, did as
" the angel of the Lord
" had bidden him, and
" took unto him his wife."
Matthew, chap 1. ver. 24.

A Saint.

An Angel.

fion, and that of Mary and Jofeph offering be fixed in the lower, then would the difpofition of the Paintings of this Window correfpond with the order of the reft.—But of the propriety of fuch a change let the reader judge when he has perufed the following pages.

☞ *The colouring of this Window is remarkably faint, tho' clear*

UPPER DIVISION.

Left Side.	Right Side.

The temptation of Eve.*

" And the serpent said un-
" to the woman, Ye shall not
" surely die. For God doth
" know, that in the day ye
" eat thereof, then your eyes
" shall be opened and ye
" shall be as Gods, knowing
" good and evil "

Gen. iii. 4, 5

**God appearing to Mo-
ses in the burning bush †**

" And the Angel of the
" Lord appeared unto him
" in a flame of fire out of the
" midst of a bush "

Exod. iii. 2

LOWER DIVISION.

**The Salutation of the
Virgin Mary, ***

" And the Angel came in
" unto her, and said, Hail
" thou that art highly fa-
" voured, the Lord is with
" thee blessed art thou a-
" mong women "

Luke i 28.

The Birth of Christ †

" And she brought forth
" her first-born son, and
" wrapped him in swadling
" clothes, and laid him in a
" manger, because there was
" no room for them in the
" inn."

Luke ii 7

* As the temptation of
Eve was the forerunner of
a general curse , so the salutation of Mary was the
forerunner of a general
blessing.

† Here is set forth the
first appearance of Moses
the deliverer of the Israelites, and the first appearance of Christ the Saviour
of the world.

*The reader, by comparing the description of a Painting in the
upper part of one Column of a leaf with the description in the
lower part of the same column, will easily form conclusions of this
kind.*

UPPER DIVISION.

Left Side.	*Right Side.*
The ceremony of circumcision first performed by Abraham.	The Queen of Sheba offering presents to King Solomon.

" And Abraham took e- " very male of his house, " and circumcised the flesh " of their fore-skin, in the " self same day as God had " said unto him " Gen xvii. 23.	" And she gave the King " an hundred and twenty ta- " lents of gold, and of spices " very great store, and pre- " cious stones." I Kings x 10

LOWER DIVISION.

The circumcision of our Saviour	The Wise-men offering gifts to Christ.

" And when eight days " were accomplished for the " circumcising of the child, " his name was called Jesus " Luke ii. 21	" And when they had o- " pened their treasures, they " presented unto him gifts ; " gold, frankincense, and " myrrh " Matth. ii 11.

UPPER DIVISION.

Left Side	Right Side.
The inftitution of the Purification of women.	Jacob, to avoid the fury of Efau, is fent to Haran

" And when the days of
" her purifying are fulfilled,
" for a fon, or for a daugh-
" ter, fhe fhall bring a lamb
" of the firft year for a burnt-
" offering, and a young pi-
" geon or a turtle-dove for a
" fin-offering, &c."
Levit xii. 6

" And Rebekah called
" Jacob her younger fon, and
" faid unto him, Behold, thy
" brother Efau, as touching
" thee, doth comfort himfelf,
" purpofing to kill thee —
" Flee thou to Laban my
" brother to Haran "
Gen xxvii. 42, 43

LOWER DIVISION.

The Purification of the Virgin Mary.	Jofeph, to avoid the fury of Herod, travels with Chrift into Egypt.

" And when the days of
" her purification, according
" to the law of Mofes, were
" accomplifhed, they brought
" him to Jerufalem, to pre-
" fent him to the Lord And
" to offer a facrifice accord-
" ing to that which is faid in
" the law of the Lord, A pair
" of turtle-doves, or two
" young pigeons "
Luke ii. 22, 24.

" Then he arofe, and took
" the young child and his
" mother by night, and de-
" parted into Egypt "
Matth. ii 14

UPPER DIVISION.

Left Side.	*Right Side.*
The children of Ifrael worfhipping (an image) the molten calf	Pharaoh's cruelty towards the Hebrew children

Left Side.

The children of Ifrael worfhipping (an image) the molten calf

" And it came to pafs as
" foon as he came nigh unto
" the camp, that he faw the
" calf, and the dancing "
Exod. xxxii. 19

Right Side.

Pharaoh's cruelty towards the Hebrew children

" And Pharaoh charged
" all his people, faying, E-
" very fon that is born ye
" fhall caft into the river,
" and every daughter ye fhall
" fave alive."
Exod. i. 22.

LOWER DIVISION.

Simeon blefling (a real God) Chrift in the Temple

" Then took he him up
" in his arms, and bleffed
" God, and faid, Lord, now
" letteft thou thy fervant de-
" part in peace, according
" to thy word "
Luke ii 28, 29.

Herod's cruelty towards the Jewifh children.

" Then Herod fent forth,
" and flew all the children
" that were in Bethlehem,
" and in all the coafts there-
" of, from two years old
" and under."
Matth. ii. 16.

UPPER DIVISION.

Left Side.

Naaman wafhing in Jordan, whereby he was eleanfed from his leprofy.*

" Then went he down and
" dipped himfelf feven times
" in Jordan, according to the
" faying of the man of God
" and his flefh came again
" like unto the flefh of a lit-
" tle child, and he was
" clean "

2 Kings v 14

Right Side

Efau tempted to fell his birth-right ‡

" And Jacob faid, Sell me
" this day thy birth-right
" And Efau faid, Behold I
" am at the point to die
" and what profit fhall this
" birth-right do to me?"

Gen. xxv 31, 32

LOWER DIVISION.

Chrift baptized by St John in Jordan.*

" Then he fuffered him
" *(to be baptized)* And
" Jefus, when he was bap-
" tized, went up ftraightway
" out of the water and lo,
" the heavens were opened
" unto him, and he faw the
" Spirit of God, defcending
" like a dove, and lighting
" upon him "

Matth. iii 15, 16

Chrift tempted in the wildernefs ‡

" Then was Jefus led up
" of the fpirit into the wil-
" dernefs, to be tempted of
" the devil.—He fetieth him
" on a pinnacle of the tem-
" ple—taketh him up into
" an exceeding high moun-
" tain."

Math. iv 1, 5, 8

* By Baptifm, or dipping into water, man is cleanfed from his fins, as Naaman was from his leprofy.

‡ Hence we may draw a reflection on the weaknefs of man in refifting temptation, without the affiftance of divine grace.

UPPER DIVISION

Left Side.

Elisha raising the Son of the Shunamite.

"And he went up, and
"lay upon the child, and
"put his mouth upon his
"mouth, and his eyes upon
"his eyes, and his hands
"upon his hands, and he
"stretched himself upon the
"child, and the child waxed
"warm————and the child
"neesed seven times, and
"the child opened his eyes"
2 Kings iv 34, 35.

Right Side

David returning from battle in triumph, with the head of Goliath.——Women meeting him and playing on their harps

"And it came to pass as
"they came, when David
"was returned from the
"slaughter of the Philistine,
"that the women came out
"of all the cities of Israel,
"singing and dancing, to
"meet King Saul, with ta-
"brets, with joy, and with
"instruments of musick.——
"And they played and said,
"Saul hath slain his thou-
"sands, and David his ten
"thousands"
1 Sam. xviii. 6, 7.

LOWER DIVISION

Christ raising Lazarus from the dead

"And when he had thus
"spoken, he cried with a
"loud voice, Lazarus, come
"forth."
John xi 43.

Christ riding in triumph to Jerusalem.——Zaccheus mounted on a tree

"And many spread their
"garments in the way. and
"others cut down branches
"off the trees, and strewed
"them in the way. And
"they that went before, and
"they that followed, cried,
"saying, Hosanna, blessed is
"he that cometh in the name
"of the Lord."
Mark xi. 8, 9.

G

UPPER DIVISION

Left Side.

Manna falling from heaven for the murmuring Ifraelites

" And when the children
" of Iſrael ſaw it, they ſaid
" one to another, It is man-
" na—And Moſes ſaid unto
" them, This is the bread
" which the Lord hath given
" you to eat "

Exod xvi 15

Right Side.

The caſting down of the rebellious Angels ‡

" For it God ſpared not
" the Angels that ſinned,
" but caſt them down to
" hell, and delivered them
" into chains of darkneſs, to
" be reſerved unto judg
" ment, &c "

2 Pet ii 4

LOWER DIVISION

The laſt ſupper * of our Lord.

" And as they did eat, Je
" ſus took bread, and bleſſed,
" and brake it, and gave to
" them, and ſaid, Take, eat
" this is my body "

Mark xiv 22

" And when he had dip-
" ped the ſop, he gave it to
" Judas Iſcariot "

John xiii 26

* Which is our heavenly food, as Manna was that of the Iſraelites

Our Saviour praying in the garden : and the Apoſtles aſleep ‡

" And being in an agon,
" he prayed more earneſtl}
" and his ſweat was as it
" were great drops of blood
" falling down to the
" ground "

Luke xxii 44

‡ The relation, which theſe two paintings bear to one another, ſeems diſcoverable only in this point, viz a breach of duty; of which both the Angels and Apoſtles were guilty the former rebelling againſt the Almighty, the latter ſleeping at the very time they were commanded to watch.—But this correſpondence, I confeſs, is by no means exact.

Left Side.

Cain, the first murder er, slaying his brother Abel.

" And it came to pass
" when they were in the
" field, that Cain rose up a-
" gainst Abel his brother,
" and slew him."

Gen. iv. 8

Right Side.

Noah drunken with new wine ——One of his sons casting a garment over him.

" And Noah began to be
" an husbandman, and he
" planted a vineyard And
" he drank of the wine, and
" was drunken, and he was
" uncovered within his tent.
" And Ham saw the naked-
" ness of his father And
" Shem and Japheth took a
" garment, and laid it upon
" both their shoulders, and
" covered the nakedness of
" their father "

Gen. ix. 20—23

LOWER DIVISION.

Judas the first betrayer of Christ, and the instrument of his death ——Peter smiting the High-Priest's servant

" And while he yet spake,
" behold, a multitude, and
" he that was called Judas,
" one of the twelve, went be-
" fore them, and drew near
" unto Jesus, to kiss him ——
" And one of them smote the
" servant of the High-Priest,
" and cut off his right ear."

Luke xxii. 47, 50

Christ bound and blind-folded.

" And when they had
" blindfolded him, they struck
" him on the face, and asked
" him, saying, Prophesy, who
" is it that struck thee ?

Luke xxii. 64.

☞ Ham discovered his father's nakedness to his brethren ——-As Noah, therefore, was unworthily treated by his own son, Ham , so was Christ un-worthily treated by his own people, the Jews.

G 2

UPPER DIVISION.

Left Side.

Jeremiah imprisoned by King Zedekiah

" Wherefore the Princes
" were wroth with Jeremiah,
" and smote him, and put
" him in prison in the house
" of Jonathan the scribe,
" for they had made that the
" prison "

Jerem. xxxvii 15

Right Side.

Shimei cursing King David *

" And thus said Shimei
" when he cursed, Come
" out, come out, thou bloody
" man, and thou man of Be-
" lial "

2 Sam. xvi 7.

LOWER DIVISION.

Christ (a prisoner) before Caiaphas, the High-Priest

" And they that had laid
" hold on Jesus, led him a-
" way to Caiaphas, the High-
" Priest, where the scribes
" and the elders were assem-
" bled "

Matth. xxvi. 57.

The soldiers mocking Christ before Herod *

" And Herod with his
" men of war set him at
" nought, and mocked him,
" and arrayed him in a gor-
" geous robe, and sent him
" again unto Pilate "

Luke xxiii. 11.

* The correspondence lies in the circumstance of *ill treatment*, which both Christ and David received.

UPPER DIVISION.

Left Side.	*Right Side.*
Job tempted by Satan, and his wife. *	Christ's espousals to the Church. †

" So Satan went forth from " the presence of the Lord, " and smote Job with sore " boils, from the sole of his " foot unto his crown Then " said his wife unto him, " Dost thou still retain thine " integrity ? curse God, and " die " Job ii 7, 9	" Go forth, O ye daugh- " ters of Sion, and behold " King Solomon with the " crown wherewith his mo- " ther crowned him in the " day of his espousals, and " in the day of the gladness " of his heart " Solomon's Song, iii 11.

LOWER DIVISION.

Christ crowned with thorns * " And they cloathed him " with purple, and platted " a crown of thorns, and put " it about his head " Mark xv 17	Christ scourged. † " And when he had " scourged Jesus, he deli- " vered him to be crucified." Matth xxvii 26

† The correspondence between these two pieces of painting appears not by any means clear ——I therefore think it better to pass over the connec- tion (whatever it may be) in silence ; than, by at- tempting an explanation, to produce an allusion ex- ceedingly distant, if not absurd.

* Here we may com- pare Job's patience under his calamities with that of Christ's under his suffer- ings.

THIS Window (which has no Meſſengers) contains circumſtances ſelected from the New Teſtament only.

IN treating on the Paintings of this Window, we muſt begin, contrary to our uſual method, by explaining the lower diviſion firſt, for the ſake of purſuing regularly the Hiſtory of Chriſt.

LOWER DIVISION.

The three Lights on the Left.

Chriſt brought to his trial.

" And Jeſus ſtood before the governor ; and the governor
' aſked him, ſaying, Art thou the King of the Jews ? And
" Jeſus ſaid unto him, Thou ſayeſt."

Matth. xxvii. 11

The three Middle Lights.

Pilate pronouncing ſentence on our Saviour, and declaring himſelf innocent of his blood, by waſhing his hands

" When Pilate ſaw that he could prevail nothing, but that
" rather a tumult was made, he took water, and waſhed his
" hands before the multitude, ſaying, I am innocent of the
" blood of this juſt perſon ſee ye to it."

Matth xxvii 24.

The three Lights on the Right.

Our Saviour bearing his Croſs.

" And he bearing his croſs, went forth into a place called
" the place of a ſkull, which is called in the Hebrew, Gol
' gotha "

John xix. 17.

UPPER DIVISION.

The three Lights on the Left.

The ſtripping and nailing of Chriſt to the Croſs.

" And they parted his garments "

Matth xxvii 35.

" They pierced my hands and my feet "
See the Prophecy of David, Pſalm xxii 17.

The three Middle Lights

Chriſt crucified between two thieves The ſoldiers caſting lots for his coat.

" And with him they crucified two thieves, the one on
" his right hand, and the other on his left "

Mark xv 27.

" Now the coat was without ſeam, woven from the top
" throughout They ſaid therefore among themſelves, Let
" us not rend it, but caſt lots for it, whoſe it ſhall be."

John xix 24.

The three Lights on the Right.

Joſeph of Arimathea taking down Chriſt from the croſs
" This man went to Pilate, and begged the body of
" Jeſus. And he took it down "

Luke xxiii 52, 53.

We now proceed to take a ſurvey of the Windows on the South ſide: on the lower and part of the upper diviſions of which is continued the Hiſtory of the New Teſtament, from the death of Chriſt to the publication of the Goſpel. And firſt, of the left ſide.

Left Side

The lamentation of Mary Magdalene and others for the death of Chrift.

" And the women alfo,
" which came with him from
" Galilee, followed after,
" and beheld the fepulcre,
" and how his body was
" laid "

Luke xxiii. 55

Right Side.

The lamentation of Naomi and her daughters for the death of their hufbands

" And the woman was
" left of her two fons, and
" her hufband —And Nao
" mi faid unto her daughters
" in law, The Lord gran
" you that you may find
" reft, each of you in the
" houfe of her hufband
" Then fhe kiffed them and
" they lift up their voice and
" wept "

Ruth 1 5, 8, 9,

HAD the Founder been ever able to execute his defign, the roof of his College would have been fixed juft under this Window; which is but half as large in length as the others, having only five *upper* Columns. Therefore it was never intended that a greater part of it fhould be glazed, than what is finifhed at prefent.— See page 9 about the intended College.

UPPER DIVISION.

Left Side

Joseph caſt into a PIT by his brethren

" And Reuben ſaid unto
" them, Shed no blood, but
" caſt him into this pit —
" And they took him, and
" caſt him into a pit."

Gen xxxvii 22, 24

Right Side.

The paſſage of the Iſraelites from Egyptian ſlavery *

" And it came to paſs the
" ſelf ſame day, that the
" Lord did bring the chil-
" dren of Iſrael out of the
" land of Eygpt by their ar-
" mies "   Exod xii. 51.

LOWER DIVISION

Chriſt laid in his GRAVE by Joseph of Arimathea ‡

" And when Joſeph had
" taken the body, he wrap-
' ped it in a clean linen cloth,
" and laid it in his own tomb,
" which he had hewn out of
" the rock "

Matth xxvii 59, 60

The paſſage of Chriſt into the region of departed ſouls, who are repreſent-ed as kneeling to him *

" Chriſt was put to death
" in the fleſh, but quickened
' by the ſpirit, by which
" alſo he went and preached
" unto the ſpirits in priſon,
" which ſometimes were diſ-
" obedient, when once the
" long - ſuffering of God
" waited in the days of No-
" ah, while the ark was a
" preparing " †

1 Pet iii 18—20.

* Moſes delivered the Iſraelites from Egyptian ſlavery.   Chriſt made known to the departed ſouls their deliverance, through his death, from the fatal conſequences of ſin —The former, there-fore, were reſcued from ſlavery, the latter from death.

‡ This Painting ſhould have preceded, in the order of the windows, Mary Mag-dalene's lamentation, for ſhe is repreſented as weeping o-ver Chriſt already laid in his grave

† This was, no doubt, the paſſage of Scripture, which the perſon, who deſigned the Painting, had in view, though he (as well as all other fa-vourers of Popery) has ſtrangely miſapplied it

H

UPPER DIVISION.

Left Side.

Jonah, after having laid in it three days and three nights, coming forth from the whale's belly.

" And the Lord fpake un-
" to the fifh, and it vomited
" out Jonah upon the dry
" land "

Jonah ii. 10.

Right Side.

The Angel difcovering himfelf to Tobit and Tobias.

" I am Raphael, one of
" the feven holy Angels,
" which prefent the prayers
" of the Saints, and which
" go in and out before the
" glory of the Holy One "

Tobit xii. 15.

LOWER DIVISION.

Chrift, after that his body had laid three days and three nights in the earth, rifing from the dead The foldiers keeping watch around the fepulcre.

" He is rifen, he is not
" here "

Mark xvi 6

" This Jefus hath God
" raifed up "

Acts ii 32.

Jefus difcovering himfelf, after his refurrection, to Mary Magdalen *

' Now when Jefus was ri-
" fen early, the firft day of
" the week, he appeared firft
" to Mary Magdalene, out
" of whom he had caft feven
" devils "

Mark xvi 9

* The place of this Painting, as well as of fome others that follow, does not ftrictly correfpond with that order, in which the facts are related by the Evangelifts.

UPPER DIVISION.

Left Side.

Reuben coming to the pit to seek for his brother Joseph.

" And Reuben returned
" unto the pit , and behold,
" Joseph was not in the pit
" and he rent his clothes."

Gen xxvii. 29

Right Side.

Daniel in the Lion's den, and King Darius amazed at finding him alive *

" And he came to the den,
" and said, O Daniel, ser-
" vant of the living God,
" is thy God whom thou
" servest continually, able to
" deliver thee from the li-
" ons ? Then said Daniel,
" My God hath sent his an-
" gel, and shut the lions
" mouths, that they have not
" hurt me "

Dan vi 20, 22.

LOWER DIVISION.

The women going to the sepulcre to seek for Jesus, and to anoint his body

" And when the sabbath
" was past, Mary Magdalene,
" and Mary the mother of
" James and Salome, had
" bought sweet spices, that
" that they might come and
" anoint him."

Mark xvi. 1.

Mary Magdalene mista-king our Saviour for the gardener. *

" She, supposing him to
" be the gardener, saith unto
" him, Sir if thou hast borne
" him hence, tell me where
" thou hast laid him, and I
" will take him away."

John xx. 15.

* Both Darius and Mary go to seek for persons whom they believed no longer surviving ; and both find them still alive.

H 2

UPPER DIVISION.

Left Side.

An Angel appearing to Habakkuk.

" Then the Angel of the
" Lord said unto Habakkuk,
" Go carry the dinner that
" thou hast into Babylon un-
" to Daniel, who is in the
" lion's den "

Hist of Bel and Dragon,
ver 34

Right Side.

An Angel holding Ha-
bakkuk by the hair over
the lion's den *

" Then the Angel of the
" Lord took him by the
" crown, and bare him by
" the hair of his head, and
" through the vehemency of
" his spirit, set him in Baby
" lon over the den. And
" Habakkuk said, O Da
" niel, Daniel, take the din
" ner which God hath sen
" thee "

Hist of Bel and Dragon,
ver 36, 37

LOWER DIVISION.

Christ appearing to two
of his disciples in the way
to Emmaus.

" After that, he appeared
" in another form unto two
" of them as they walked,
" and went into the coun-
" try."

Mark xvi. 12

Christ breaking bread
to two of his disciples at
Emmaus *

" And it came to pass, as
" he sat at meat with them,
" he took bread, and blessed
" it, and break, and gave to
" them "

Luke xxiv 30.

* The correspondence
probably depends on this
circumstance, viz admini-
stering food Habakkuk
feeds Daniel Christ distri-
butes bread to two of his
disciples.

UPPER DIVISION

Left Side.

The prodigal fon acknowledging and giving up his licentious life.*

" And the fon faid unto
" him, Father, I have finned
" againft heaven, and before
" thee, and am no more
" worthy to be called thy
" fon."

Luke xv 21, 22.

Right Side.

Jofeph meeting his father and brethren in Egypt.

" And Jofeph went up to
" meet Ifrael his father, to
" Gofhen, and prefented
" himfelf unto him. and he
" fell on his neck, and wept
" on his neck a good while."

Gen. xlii 29.

LOWER DIVISIO.

Thomas acknowledging and giving up his incredulity

' Then faith he unto Tho
" mas, Reach hither thy fin-
" ger, and behold my hands
" And Thomas anfwered
" and faid unto him, My
" Lord, and my God."

John xx 27, 28

Chrift appearing to his eleven Apoftles.

" Afterward he appeared
" unto the eleven, as they
" fat at meat, and upbraided
" them with their unbelief,
" and hardnefs of he^rt, be-
" caufe they believed not
" them which had feen him
" after he was rifen "

Mark xvi 24

* This painting is taken from the New Teftament, contrary to the preceding ones in the upper parts of the Windows.

UPPER DIVISION.

Left Side.

Elijah taken up into heaven in a chariot of fire, and Elisha catching his mantle

" Behold, there appeared
" a chariot of fire, and part
" ed them both asunder,
" and Elijah went up by a
" whirlwind into heaven —
" He took up also the mantle
" of Elijah "

2 Kings ii 11, 13

Right Side.

The law given to Moses from Sinai.—Some of the Israelites fallen on their faces at the foot of the mountain *

" And he gave unto Mo
" ses, when he had made an
" end of communing with
" him upon Mount Sinai, two
" tables of testimony, tables
" of stone."

Exod xxxi. 18

LOWER DIVISION.

Christ ascending into heaven

" And when he had spoken
" these things, while they be-
" held, he was taken up, and
" and a cloud received him
" out of their sight "

The Holy Ghost given to the Apostles *

" And there appeared unto
" them, cloven tongues, like
" as of fire, and it sat upon
" each of them and they
" were all filled with the Ho-
" ly Ghost, and began to speak
" with other tongues "

Acts ii 3, 4.

* In these Paintings we may observe the different circumstances that attended the promulgation of the *Old* Law and the *New* the former being delivered in terror and thundering, the latter in mercy and peace.

⁎ This Window is by most people adjudged to be the most beautiful about the Chapel, the Eastern Window excepted

From this Window the Paintings in the upper divisions bear no relation to those in the lower.

UPPER DIVISION.

Left Side

Peter and John reftoring a lame man to his feet at the Beautiful gate of the temple.

" Then Peter fa d, Silver
" and gold have I none, but
" fuch as I have give I thee
" In the name of Jefus Chrift
" of Nazareth, rife up and
" walk."

Acts iii. 6.

Right Side.

The imprifonment and beating of Peter and John.

" A d the High-Prieft and
" all they that were with him
" laid their hands upon the
" Apoftles, and put them in
" the common prifon And
" when they had called the
" Apoftles, and beaten them,
" they commanded that they
" fhould not fpeak in the
" name of Jefus, and let
" them go "

Acts v. 17, 18, 20.

LOWER DIVISION

The beggar reftored to the ufe of his feet, walking before Peter and John towards the temple

" And he leaping up ftood
" and walked, and entered
" with them into the tem-
" ple."

Acts iii 8, 12.

The death of Ananias *

" And Ananias, hearing
" thefe words, fell down, and
" gave up the ghoft."

Acts v. 5.

In the back-ground there is a fmall figure of Peter preaching to the people, whom the report of his miracle had brought together.

* The figure of Ananias expiring is fo well executed, that it will bear the ftricteft examination.

UPPER DIVISION.

Left Side

The converfion of St. Paul.

" And he fell to the earth,
" and heard a voice faving
" unto him, Saul, Saul, why
" perfecuteft thou me ?"

Acts IX 4

Right Side.

Paul preaching and dif-puting at Damafcus ——A fmall figure of Paul, whom the difciples are letting down from the walls of Damafcus in a basket

" But Saul increafed the
" more in ftrength, and con
" founded the Jews which
" dwelt at Damafcus ——
" Straightway he preached
" Chrift ——And after mar
" days the Jews took counfel
" to kill him, watching the
" gates day and night Then
" the difciples took him by
" night, and let him down by
" the wall in a bafket "

Acts IX 20, 2,

LOWER DIVISION.

Paul and Barnabas re-verenced as Gods ——A vic tim brought before them.

" And when the people
" faw what Paul had done,
" they lift up their voices,
" faving, in the fpeech of Ly-
" caonia, The Gods are
" come down to us in the
" likenefs of men "

Acts XIV, 11,

Paul ftoned

" And there came thither
" certain Jews from Antioca
" and Iconium, who perfua-
" ded the people, and having
" ftoned Paul, drew him out
' of the city, fuppofing he
" had been dead "

Acts XIV 19

UPPER DIVISION

Left Side.

Paul cafting out a fpirit of divination from a woman.—A figure intended for the fpirit.

" A certain damfel, pof-
" feffed with a fpirit of di-
" vination, met us, which
" brought her mafters much
" gain by foothfaying. The
" fame followed us many
" days But Paul being
" grieved faid to the fpirit,
" I command thee in the
" name of Jefus Chrift to
" come out of her And he
" came out the fame hour."

Acts xvi. 16—18.

Right Side

Paul before King Agrippa

" I think myfelf happy,
" King Agrippa, becaufe I
" fhall anfwer for myfelf this
" day before thee, touching
" all the things whereof I am
" accufed of the Jews "

Acts xxvi. 2.

LOWER DIVISION.

Paul's friends diffuading him from his intended journey to Jerufalem A young woman (probably one of Philip's daughters, who was a prophetefs) kneeling at his feet.——A very beautiful figure of a fhip, reprefenting the veffel in which Paul had fail'd from Ptolemais to Cæfarea in Paleftine

' We entered the houfe of
" Philip the Evangelift.—
" The fame man had four

Paul before the Roman governor Felix.

" Then Paul, after that
" the governor had beckoned
" unto him to fpeak, an-
" fwered, Forafmuch as I
" know that thou haft been
" many years a judge unto
" this nation, I do the more
" cheerfully anfwer for my-
" felf."

Acts xxiv. 10.

" daughters, virgins which did prophefy —And both we,
" and they of that place, befought him not to go up to Jeru-
" falem Then Paul anfwered, What mean ye to weep, and
" to break mine heart ? for I am ready not to be bound only,
" but alfo to die at Jerufalem, for the name of the Lord Jefus."

I   Acts xxi. 8—13.

WHATEVER the idea be, which the reader may have formed of thefe hiftorical Paintings, it will (I may venture to affirm) fall fhort of their exceffive beauty. For, in the greater part of them, the fhape and attitude of particular figures, the fitnefs and expreffion of their feveral countenances, and the colouring and flowing of their drapery, are all wonderfully natural, and far beyond the limits of defcription

I fhall briefly take notice of the fervice of the Chapel and difmifs the fubject of this complete Building of Gothic architecture.

ON every day throughout the year (excepting the Sabbath and holy days) divine fervice is performed in the Chapel three times In the morning twice. Early prayers are read at a quarter before feven, intended chiefly for the Scholars. There is likewife cathedral fervice at ten ; and cathedral fervice at five in the afternoon. On Sundays and Saints days, there is only cathedral fervice in the morning at eight and at four in the afternoon. On the eves too of thefe days the fervice is at four in the afternoon But if on Sunday or other holy day the facrament is to be adminiftered, there is cathedral fervice and a fermon at ten.

ON the twenty-fifth day of March, at eleven in the morning, (which is a grand feaft in honour of the Virgin Mary, to whom the Chapel is dedicated) a fermon is preached in the Chapel by one of the Fellows of the College, which the whole Univerfity, inftead of going to St. Mary's church, as ufual, on that day attends.

A
LIST of the PROVOSTS, &c.

TO the following Lift, which is drawn from Fuller's Church-Hiftory, I fhall prefix, by way of introduction, a paffage from that Author Having fpoken of the meannefs of the prefent old fquare, he thus proceeds.

" But the honour of Athens lyeth not in her walls,
" but in the worth of her citizens. Building may give
" luftre, but learning life to a Colledge; wherein we
" congratulate the happinefs of this foundation. Indeed no Colledge can continue in a conftant *level of*
" *learning*, but will have it's alternate *depreffions* and
" *elevations* but in this we may obferve a *good tenor*
" of able men in all faculties, as indeed a *good Artift* is
" left-handed to no profeffion. See here their Catalogue."

PROVOSTS.

1. William Millington, elected *anno* 1444, from Clare Hall, whither, after three years, he was remanded, for his factious endeavouring to prefer his countrymen of Yorkfhire.

2 John Chedworth, who continued fix years.

3. Richard Woodlark, D. D. Founder of Katherine Hall

4 Walter Field, D. D. elected 1479, continued 20 years

5. John Dogget, D C L Chancellor of Sarum, elected 1499, and remained fo two years

6. John Argentine, D. P and D. (He gave the College a fair bafon and ewer of filver, yet in the cuftody of the Provoft) elected 1501, and remained fix years.   I 2   7. Richard

7. Richard Hutton, D. C. L. elected 1507, continued two years

8. Robert Hacomblen, D. D. elected 1509, and remained 19 years. He wrote Comments on Aristotle's Ethicks

9 Edward Fox, afterward Bishop of Hereford, elected 1538, and continued ten years.

10 George Day, afterward Bishop of Chichester, elected 1528, and continued ten years.

11. Sir John Cheek, (of St. John's in Cambridge) chosen by mandate 1548, sate five years.

12. Richard Atkinson, D D. elected 1553, so remained three years

13. Robert Braffey, chosen 1556, and so remained two years

14. Philip Baker, chosen 1558, sate 14 years.

15 Roger Goad, a grave and reverend Divine, elected 1570, and remained Provost 40 years. He gave the rectory of Milton in Cambridgeshire to the Colledge

16. Fog Newton, D. D chosen 1610, sate two years

17 William Smith, chosen 1612, two years.

18. Samuel Collins, chosen 1615, continued 30 years

19 Benjamin Whichcot, elected 1645, sat 15 years

20 James Fletewood, D. D. 1660, continued 15 years.

21. Thomas Page, Knt. chosen 1675, continued six years.

22. John Copleftone, D. D. elected 1681, continued eight years.

23. Charles Roderick, D. D. chosen 1689, sat 22 years

24. John Adams, D. D chosen 1712, sat seven years.

25 Andrew Snape, D. D chosen 1719, sat 22 years

26 William George, first Canon of Windsor, then Dean of Lincoln, elected 1742

27. John Sumner, D. D. and Canon of Windsor, elected 1756.

BISHOPS.

1. Nicholas Cloofe, ⎰ Carlifle.
      1451.   ⎱ Litchfield.

2. John Chedworth, Bifhop of Lincoln, 1452.

3. Thomas Rotherham, Rochefter firft, then Lincoln, then York, 1467. Chancellor of Cambridge, and Lord High Chancellor of England.

4 Oliver King, Exeter, then Bath and Wells, 1492.

5. Jeffery Blith, 1503, Coventrie and Litchfield.

6. Nicolas Weft, when Scholar of this Houfe, fo defperately turbulent, that difcontented with the lofs of the Proctorfhip, he endeavoured to fire the Provoft's lodgings, and, having ftolen fome filver fpoons, departed the College. Afterward he became a new man, D D and Bifhop of Elie, (1515) who, to expiate his former faults, gave many rich gifts and plate to the Colledge, and built part of the Provoft's lodgings.

7 Nicolas Hawkins, 1533, nominated Bifhop of Elie, but died before his confecration. In time of famine he fold all his plate and goods to relieve the poor of Elie, where he was ferved himfelf in wooden difhes and earthen pots.

8. Thomas Goodrich, 1534, Elie.

9. Edward Fox, 1535, Hereford

10. Robert Aldrich, 1537, Carlifle ——Erafmus ftyleth him when young, *Blandæ eloquentiæ juvenem*, a young man of engaging eloquence.

11. George Day, 1543, Chichefter. He was one of the compilers of our Liturgy

12. John Poinet, 1550, Rochefter, then Winchefter.

13 Richard Cox, 1559, Elie Scholar of this Houfe.

14 Edmund Gweft, 1559, Rochefter, then Sarum.

15 William Alley, 1560, Exeter.

16 William Wickam, 1595, Lincoln, then Winchefter

17. Thomas Ram, Bifhop of Ferns in Ireland.

18. Richard Mountague, 1628, Chichefter, then Norwich

19 John Long, Armagh, fome thirty years fince, not finding the date of his confecration.

                         20. William

20. William Murrey, Conduct of this Colledge, Bi
ſhop of Landaff, *anno* 1627.

21. John Pearſon, conſecrated Biſhop of Cheſter,
1672.

22 James Fleetwood, conſecrated Biſhop of Wor
ceſter, 1673.

STATESMEN.

1. William Hatliffe, D. D. Secretarie to King Edward the Fourth.

2. James Denton, D C. L. Chancellor to the Lady
Mary Dowager of France, Dean of Litchfield, and Lord
Preſident of Wales

3. William Coniſby, became a ſtudent of the common law, and a learned judge.

4. Edward Hall, afterward a judge, and a uſeful
hiſtorian.

5 Walter Haddon, Maſter of the Requeſts to Queen
Elizabeth

6. Ralph Colfield, Clerk of the Council in Wales
to King Edward the Sixth.—He diſcovered the cheat-
ing of dicers

7 Thomas Wilſon, principal Secretarie to Queen
Elizabeth.

8 Giles Fletcher, Ambaſſador for Queen Elizabeth
into Ruſſia, Commiſſioner into Scotland, Germanie,
and the Low-Countries

9. Thomas Ridley, Doctor of Law, Maſter of the
Chancery, Knight and Vicar-General

10 John Oſburne, Remembrancer to the Treaſurer.
He never took fee of any Clergyman

11. Joſeph Jeſop, Secretarie to Secretarie Walſingham.

12 Sir Albert Morton, principal Secretarie to King
James.

Sir Robert Walpole, a character that deſerves the
higheſt veneration

Theſe Stateſmen were of the Foundation

Sir Francis Walſingham, principal Secretarie of
State,

tate, was Fellow-Commoner of this Houfe; to which
e gave the King of Spain his Bible.*

LEARNED WRITERS‡

1 Thomas Stacey, and William Sutton, his fcholar :
amous Aftrologers, and Students in the old Hoftles,
f which this College was afterward compofed.
 2 Phinehas Fletcher, an eminent Poet
 3 Dr R Croke, learned in the Greek language.
 4 William Buckley, a skilful Mathematician.
 5 Dr Aldrich, a good Latin Poet.
 6 Ofmund Lake, a profound Scholar.
 7. G. Day, one of the compilers of our Liturgy.
 8. Nicholas Carre, a learned Divine
 9 Dr Hacomblen (See the Lift of Provofts)
 10 Thomas Hatcher, an eminent Antiquarian.
 11 Dr. Fox, Author *Libri de vera differentia Rega-
 li poteftatis et Ecclefiafticæ.*
 12. Dr. Cox, one of the tranflators of the Bible.
 13 Sir J Cheek, Author of many learned works.
 14 Dr. Alley, an able Preacher and Linguift, and
one of the tranflators of Queen Elizabeth's Bible
 15 John Herde.
 16 Dr Gueft.
 17. Dr Ward, a tranflator of the Bible.
 18 B Clerke wrote againft N Saunders the Jefuit.
 19 Richard Mulcafter, an eminent Grecian
 20. Thomas Thomas, Author of the Dictionary
fince called Rider's.
 21 A. Wotton, firft Prof. of Div. in Grefham Coll.
22. J.

* This Book (which Fuller had probably never feen himfelf, as he calls it a *Bible)* is a moft curious Concordance to
the *Vulgate* The leaves are made of thin, fmooth Vellum,
nicely illuminated It was (I fuppofe) prefented to the College with the Manufcript of the Pfalms See page 35.
 ‡ This Catalogue of eminent Writers, though rather inac-
curate, is yet the beft I am able to procure. It is not extracted
from Fuller, whofe Lift is exceedingly incomplete.

22. J. Cowell, Doctor of Civil Law, and eminent to posterity for his INTERPRETER and INSTITUTIONS

23 Samuel Hieron, a noted Preacher

24 Dr Sclater, a learned Divine and Commentator

25. Elnathan Parr, an industrious Writer.

26. Dr. Kellet, Author of the *Miscellanea sacra.*

27 William Whitcock, Author of *Chronicon*

28. Dr. Goade, (son of Dr Goade, Provost) one of the Divines sent to the Synod at Dort.

29. Dr Gouge.

30 Sir Thomas Ridley wrote on the Eucharist, and Ecclesiastical Laws.   He was called a general scholar.

31 Wm. Oughtred, Author *Clavis Mathematicæ.*

32. William Lisle, a learned Antiquarian.

33. Dr Wotton wrote in defence of the Com. Prayer.

34 Edm Waller, first refiner of English poetry

35. Dr Mountague, Author of many learned works.

36 Dr Whichcot, a pious Preacher and Author

37. L Rooke, eminent in Mathematics and Astron.

38. Roger Lupton.

39. Dr. Hyde, assistant to Dr. Walton in the Poly-glot-Bible

40. Dr Pearson, most famous for his Exposition of the Apostle's Creed.

41. Dr. Hatclyffe wrote against Popery.

42. William Bowles wrote several Poems

43. Dr Wittie, M D. wrote on Mineral Waters

44. John Taylor, Translator of Valerius Maximus.

45 Dr Price, Author of the Mystery and Method of the King's happy restoration.

46 Dr Ghest, a learned Writer against the Papists and Puritans

47. Dr. Fleetwood, Author of the relative duties.

48 Henry Jones, an abridger of the Philosophical Transactions.

49. Anthony Collins, noted for his writings in favour of Free-thinkers

50. Dr Stanhope, Author of the Paraphrase, &c on the Epistles and Gospels

51. Dr.

51. Dr Lyttleton, an elegant Preacher and Poet.

52. Dr. Hare published an edition of Terence, and something from Job

53. Dr. King, editor of Euripides.

54. Dr Andrew Snape, engaged in the controversy against the Bishop of Bangor.

55. Dr. Weston, an eminent Preacher.

MARTYRS and CONFESSORS.

1. John Frith, first a Student in this Colledge (but not of the foundation) burnt for the testimony of the truth in 1533. 1. Q. Mary

2 Laurence Saunders suffered for the same in 1555.

3 Robert Glover, burnt at Coventrie for religion.

4 John Hullier, martyred in the reign of Mary, on Jesus-Green in Cambridge, for writing an Essay on the Common-Prayer

5 Robert Columbel, Confessor; he went away Fellow, not daring to stay, because Mr Stokis * (the Beadle) had espied a Latin Testament in his hand.

6. Thomas Whitehead, Scholar, and afterward Panmen of the College. When Luther's books were sought to be burnt, he kept them close for better times. He was a Confessor

Thus far proceeds Fuller.

Such is the Catalogue of worthy and eminent men, who, having received the principles of their education in that renowned Nursery of Learning ETON-College, afterward completed it in this House: whose diligence in their respective employments has procured the most solid advantages to their country, has adorned it's annals, and will ever continue glorious in the memory of all posterity.

" BEHOLD

---

* The brazen monument near the South door of the Ante-Chapel was erected by him to his brother's memory in 1559.

K

" BEHOLD here (to ufe the words of Fuller) the
" fruitfulnefs of one vineyard (a fingle Colledge) and
" yet we have onely gathered the top-grapes, fuch as
" were ripeft in parts and higheft in preferment.
" How many more grew on the under-boughs, which
" were ferviceable in Church and State!"

THE Catalogue given above (except the Lift of the
Provofts and learned Writers) is continued accurately
only to 1630. As I am unable to complete it, I fhall
not attempt to extend it.

BUT rarely could a College boaft, in any age, fuch a
number of profound Scholars, diftinguifhed both in
Church and State, as can this in the prefent with
whofe confpicuous characters in their feveral profef-
fions, or learned and elegant publications, the world
is already fo well acquainted, that I fhall forbear an un-
neceffary recital. Of one, however, I would beg
leave to take particular notice : fince, from the duty I
owe the Society, I am bound to make mention of the
name at leaft of that moft illuftrious perfonage Lord
CAMDEN, the prefent Lord High Chancellor; who
was admitted Fellow of the College in 1734

I have only left further to add my hearty good-
wifhes for all increafe of welfare and happinefs to the
Members of the prefent Society : and my moft earneft
prayers, that KING's COLLEGE may always (as we
have feen it hath in the more early age of literature)
furnifh the kingdom with it's full proportion of able
and learned men; and flourifh, as at this day, to the
lateft generations.

The AUTHOR's
A P O L O G Y
AND GRATEFUL
ACKNOWLEDGMENTS
To his Subscribers.

AT length I have reached the end of my work, which, I am sensible, stands in need of no small share of the reader's indulgence. Happy indeed were it for me, if my attempt should only not displease.

However, as I could wish to escape the persecution of censure, it may not be amiss to answer two objections, which may perhaps (nor without reason) be brought against my book.

It may be said either that my description of the Chapel is not sufficiently accurate, or (which is the principal objection) that the proper execution of such a work is far beyond the compass of my abilities.

To the first I thus return.—A description of a Building is in general uninteresting , but especially when it descends to take notice of the minutest articles. I confess there are many striking pieces of work, of which I have taken no notice but these are chiefly the smallest figures, expressive features of the countenance, and other nice touches of art of the like nature. of all which description (not being fitted to such explanations) would afford but an imperfect idea It will be readily allowed, I believe, by those who have observed the different parts of the Chapel, that my book must have been spun out into a tedious and immoderate length, had I attempted to give a circumstantial detail of that

profusion

profusion of workmanship, which is bestowed even on the obscurest corners of the Building. I shall, therefore, recommend it to the more curious to gratify their sight by a closer examination of each particular

With regard to my inability in the capacity of a writer, I humbly request indulgence from the learned, and protection from all favourers of honest industry For this work has been undertaken chiefly to support me under necessitous circumstances, to which the perplexities of debt (not occasioned by my own misconduct) have long since reduced me.

It now remains that I return my sincerest thanks to those beneficent and tender hearts, which could feel with pity for my sufferings. and sympathize in the calamities of a family languishing under want, and overwhelmed in misery and affliction.—But their munificence has softened my distress, and afforded a prospect of more happy days than it hath yet been my fortune to enjoy. How deep, therefore, must be my sense of gratitude to all Subscribers, whose liberality has supplied me, amidst the horrors of indigence, with a seasonable and ample relief Their motive indeed was charity it was the effect of a generous benevolence and to commend it is become a debt of justice to them But I will not praise, but pray for them — Their bountiful contributions I better know how to value than to deserve. That I accept them most thankfully, is the only return I am able to make, and is all I am able to express. For a reward I refer each particular benefactor to the satisfaction and testimony of his own conscience ——But I will put a period to this address, and conclude with my warmest wishes, that the execution of this work may incline the reader to believe, that I have spared neither labour nor enquiry to render my performance at least not unentertaining

INDENTURES

INDENTURES.

The FIRST INDENTURE:

In which it is agreed by the contracting parties, that an inner roof of stone should be built for 1200l.

THIS INDENTURE made the   day of   in the fourth yere of our fovrain lord kyng Herry the 8th betwyne Mr. Robert Hacombleyn provoft of the kyng's college royal at Cambrydge and the fcolers of the fame with the advife and agrement of Mr. Thomas Larke furveyor of the kyng's works there on the oon partye, and John Waftell mafter mafon of the feid works, and Herry Semerk oon of the wardens of the fame on the other partye, witneffeth that hit is covenaunted bargayned and agreed betwyne the partyes aforefeid, That the feid John Waftell and Herry Semerk fhall make and fett up, or cawfe to be made and fett up at ther cofts and charges, a good, fuer, and fufficient vawte for the grete churche there, to be workmanly wrought, made, and fett up after the beft handlynge and forme of good workmanfhip, according to a plat thereof made and figned with the hands of the lords executors to the kyng of moft famous memorye Herry the 7th, whofe fowle God pardon. And the feid John Waftell and Herry Semerk fhall provide and fynde at ther coft and charges, as moche good fufficient able fton of Weldon quarryes, as fhall fuffife for the performing of all the feid vawte, together with lyme, fand, fcaffoldyng, cinctores, moles, ordinaunces, and every other thyng concerning the fame vawting, as well workmen and laborers, as all manner of ftuff and ordinaunces that fhall be required or neceffary for the performance of the fame; except the feid Mr. Provoft and fcolers with the affent of the feid furveyors granten to the feid John Waftell and Herry Semerk for the great coft and charge that they fhall be at in remevyng the grete fcaffold there, to have therefore in recompence at the end and performyng of the feid vawte the timber of two fevereyes* of the
feid

* *The whole roof of the Chapel is divided into twelve parts, (anfwering to twelve windows on either fide) the*
feparation

feid grete fcaffold by them remeved to ther own ufe and pro-
fight; And over that the feid Provoft, fcolers, and furveyor
granten that the feid John Waftell and Herry Semerk fhall
have

*feparation being made by eleven principal ribs, correfponding to
the number of buttreffes on the outfide. The fpace contained between any two of thefe ribs is, in the Indenture, called a fevery*

*This roof is fo conftructed, that it has no dependance on the
walls between buttrefs and buttrefs on either fide, or between
tower and tower at either end of the Chapel the whole weight
of the roof being fo fupported by the buttreffes and towers, that
if the above-mentioned walls fhould be entirely taken away, the
buttreffes and towers only remaining, the roof would ftill continue
as firm as it is at this hour*

*But what may juftly claim an equal degree of wonder is, that
thofe large ftones (mentioned page 24) in the center of each fevery, which may be confidered as the key-ftones of the vault, might
at any time be fafely taken out without endangering the vault it-
felf. Hence it appears, that this roof is fo geometrically contrived, that it would ftand firm without either the walls or the
key-ftones —The myftery of conftructing vaults of this kind was
the original fecret of* Free-Mafons *of whom John Waftell, the
Mafter-Mafon, contracted to employ not lefs than fixty, for carrying on the works of this Chapel —This note I am authorifed to
add by a Gentleman who has made the Structure of many ancient Gothic buildings, and particularly that of King's Chapel,
his favourite ftudy*

Of Free-Mafons, *as they were the Builders of the Chapel,
I fhall beg leave to give the following account*

A fet of Foreigners, who called themfelves FREE-MASONS,
*(becaufe none were acquainted with the fecrets of their trade, ex-
cept fuch as were* Free *and* Accepted *Members of their Society)
are faid to have introduced the art of building with ftone into
England, about the middle of the feventh century Thefe were
formerly divided into parties or companies Each company was
fubject to a* Mafter, a Warden, *and other inferior Officers (names
retained among Free-Mafons to this day) They affembled in one
common room, (called a* Lodge) *where they confulted about carrying on the works which their Mafter and Warden had undertaken for they were chiefly employed in raifing Cathedrals, Chapels, and other buildings of the like kind. A company of Free-
Mafons (as I am led to conclude from the fecond and third Indentures,*

have duryng the tyme of the ſeid vawtyng, certeyne ſtuffs and neceſſaryes there, as gynnes, whels, cables, hobynatts, ſawes, and ſuch other as ſhall be delyvered unto them by indenture; And they to delyver the ſame agayne unto the college there, at the end of the ſeid worke The ſeid John Waſtell and Herry Semerk granten alſo and bynde themſelves by theſe covenauntes, that they ſhall performe and clerely fynyſh all the ſeid vawte within the terme and ſpace of three yeres next enſuyng, after the tyme of ther begynnyng upon the ſame; And for the good and ſuer performyng of all the premyſſes as is afore ſpecyfyed, The ſeid Provoſt and ſcolers covenaunte and graunte to pay unto the ſeid John Waſtell and Herry Semerk 1200l. that is to ſey, for every ſeverey in the ſeid churche 100l to be payd in forme followyng, from tyme to tyme as moche money as ſhall ſuffiſe to pay the maſons and others rately after the numbre of workmen, And alſo for ſton in ſuche tymes and in ſuche forme as the ſeid John Waſtell
and

tures) to their immortal honour, contracted for building differ-
ent parts of the Chapel. They have left, I am told, in the courſe
of their work, certain marks very well known to all adepts of their
Society. What theſe monuments of Maſonry may be, I am unable
to declare but refer my reader, if he is learned in the ſecrets of
that fraternity, to an inſpection of every myſterious token about
the Building One thing, however, I ſhall mention, which has
often been obſerved,—that in the South Porch of the Chapel
there are THREE *ſteps, at the Weſt door* FIVE, *and in*
the North Porch SEVEN. *Theſe are numbers, with the my-*
ſtery or at leaſt with the ſound of which, Free-Maſons are ſaid
to be particularly well acquainted
    It is obſervable that, notwithſtanding the encouragement Free-
Maſons received from Henry VI by being employed in erecting his
magnificent Chapel, an act paſſed, in the third year of his reign,
for ſuppreſſing their aſſembling, or holding chapters in any part of
his dominions it being the prevailing opinion of thoſe times,
that their meetings were held for the ſake of making an extra-
vagant addition to the wages of the Working-Maſons But a
favourable report being made to his Majeſty by ſome of the Nobi-
lity, who had been admitted into the Brother-hood, he afterwards
received them into his favour, and ſhewed them marks of a
particular reſpect The act itſelf remains, I believe, as yet un-
repealed. It is, however, probable, that the perſon who was
Architect of the Chapel (ſee page 20) was a Member of that
Fraternity

and Herry Semerk fhall make ther bargaynes for fton, fo
that they be evyn paid with 100l. at the end of the performyng evry feverey; and if there remayne ony parte of the feid
100l. at the fynifhing of the faid feverey, then the feid Mr.
Provoft and fcolers to pay unto them the furplufage of the
feid 100l. for that feverey, and fo from tyme to tyme until
all the feid twelve fevereys be fully and perfyttly made and
performed.

The SECOND INDENTURE:

Concerning the vaulting of two Porches, one on each
  fide of the Chapel : and alfo feven * Chapels, (four
  on the North fide, towards the Weft , and three on
  the South fide) and nine * other Chapels behind the
  Choir, with their Battlements . 25l. to be paid for
  vaulting each of the Porches; 20l. for each of the
  feven Chapels; 12l. for each of the nine Chapels,
  and for Stone and Workmanfhip of the Battlements
  of all the faid Chapels and Porches, divided into
  twenty Sev023, each Severey 100s.

THIS INDENTURE made the fourth day of Auguft in
  the fifth yere of the reign of our fovrain lord kyng
Herry the 8th, betwyne Mr. Robert Hacombleyn Provoft of
the kyng's college royal in Cambrydge and the fcolers of
the fame with the advife and agrement of Mr. Thomas
Larke furveyor of the kyng's works there on the oon partye,
and John Waftell mafter mafon of the feid works on the other
partye, witneffeth, That it is covenannted, bargayned, and a-
greed betwyne the partyes aforefeid, that the feid John Waftell fhall make and fett up, or cawfe to be made and fett up,
at his propre coft and charge, the vawting of two porches of
the newe churche of the kyng's college aforefeid with Yorkfhere fton, And alfo the vawtes of feven chapels in the body
of the fame churche with Weldon fton, accordynge to a plat
made as well for the fame feven chapels as for the feid two
                                                              porches

---

* Thefe, with the two others, mentioned page 27, make up the
whole number of veftries on each fide of the building.

porches, and nine other chapels behynd the quyre of the feid churche with like Weldon fton to be made of a more courfe werke, as appereth by a plat for the fame made   And that the feid John Waftell fhall make and fett up or cawfe to be made and fett up at his coft and charge the batelments of all the feid porches and chapels with Weldon fton accordynge to another plat made for the fame remaynyng with all the other plats afore reherfed in the kepynge of the feid furvey or figned with the hands of the lords the kynge's executors   All the feid vawtes and batelments to be well and workmanly wrought made and fett up after the beft handlyng and forme of good workmanfhvp, and accordyng to the plats afore fpecified : The forefeid John Waftell to provide and fynde at his coft and charge not only as moche good fufficient and hable fton of Hampole quarryes in Yorkfhere as fhall fuffife for the performance of the feid two porches, but alfo as moche good fufficient and hable fton of Weldon quarryes as fhall fuffife for the performyng of all the feid chapels and batelments, together with lyme, fand, fcaffoldyng, mooles, ordinaunces, and every other thyng concernyng the fynyfhing and performyng of all the feid vawtes and batelments, as well workmen and laborers, as all maner of ftuff and ordinaunce as fhall be requyred or neceffary for performance of the fame   provided alwey that the feid John Waftell fhall kepe continually 60 fre mafons workyng upon the fame   The feid John Waftell graunteth alfo and byndeth hvmfelf by thefe prefents to performe and clerely fynyfh all the feid vawtes and batelments on this fide the ffeefte of the Nativitie of Seint John Baptifte next enfuyng after the date hereof , And for the good and fuer performyng of all thefe premyffes, as is afore fpecyfyed the feid provoft and fcolers granten to pay unto the feid John Waftell for fton and workmanfhyp of evry the feid porches with all other charge as is afore reherfed 25l.

And for evry of the feid feven chapels in the body of the churche after the plat of the feid porches 20l

And for vawtyng of evry of the other nine chapels behind the quyre to be made of more courfe work 12l

And for fton and workmanfhyp of the batelments of all the feid chapels and porches devided into twenty fevereys evry feverey at 100s fum 100l

And for all and fingler covenaunts afore reherfed of the partye of the feid John Waftell wele and truly to be performed and kept, he byndeth himfelf, his heirs and executors in 400'

L   of

of good and lawful money of England to be paid unto the
feid Mr Provoft, fcolers and furveyor at the ffeefte of the
Purification of our Bleffed Lady next comyng after the date
of thefe prefentes, and in lyke wife for all and fingler cove
nauntes afore reherfed, of the partye of the feid Mr Provoft,
fcolers and furveyor we'e and truly to be performed and kept,
they bynde themfelves, their fucceffors and executors in 400l
of good and lawfull money of England to be paid unto the
feid John Waftell at the feid ffeefte of the Purification of our
Bleffed Lady, In witneffe whereof the partyes aforefeid to thefe
prefent indentures interchangeably have fett their feals, the
day and yere above wryten.

The THIRD INDENTURE

Concerning erecting the Pinnacles of twenty-one
Buttreffes, and finifhing one of the Towers Fo[
every Pinnacle to be paid 6l 13s. 4d and for all
the faid Pinnacles 140l. and for the upper part of
the Tower (viz. from the open-work upwards) 100l

THIS INDENTURE made the fourth day of January in
the fourth yere of the reign of our foverayn lord kyng
Herrey the 8th. betwene Mr Robert Hacombleyn provoft of
the kynge's college royal in Cambrvdge and the fcolers of the
fame with the advice and agrement of Mr Thomas Larke,
furveyor of the kynge's works there on the oon partye, and
John Waftell mafter mafon of the feid works on the other par
tye witneffeth, That it is covenaunted, bargayned, and agreed
betwene the partyes aforefeid, that the feid John Waftell fhall
make and fett up, or cawfe to be made and fett up at his pro
pre cofts and charges the fynyalls of the buttraffes of the grett
cnurche there, which be 21 in numbre, the feid fynyalls to
be well and workmanly wrought made and fett up after the
beft handelyng and forme of good workmanfhyp, according
to the plats conceyved and made for the fame, and according
to the fynyall of oon buttraffe which is wrought and fett up
except that all thefe new fynyalls fhall be made fum what
larger in certayne places, according to the mooles for the
fame conceyved and made Alfo it is covenaunted, bargayned
and agreed betwene the partyes aforefeid that the feid John
Waftell fhall make and fett up or cawfe to be made and fett up

at his propre cofts and charges the fynyfhing and performyng of oon towre at oon of the corners of the feid churche, as fhall be affigned unto him by the furveyor of the feid works, all the feid fynvfhing and performyng of the feid towre with fynyalls ryfant Gabletts, batelments, orbys, or croffe quarters, and evry other thynge belongyng to the fame, to be well and workmanly wrought made and fett up after the beft handelyng and forme of good workmanfhip, accordyng to a plat thereof made remaynyng in the kepyng of the feid furveyor. The feid John Waftell to provide and fynde at his coft and charge as moche good fuffycyent and hable fton of Weldon quarryes, as fhall fuffife for the performyng of the fynyalls of all the feid buttraffes, and alfo for the performyng and tynyfhing of oon of the towres, as is afore fpecyfyed, together with ime, fand, fcaffoldyng, mooles, ordynaunces and evry other thynge concernyng the fynyfhing and performyng of all the buttraffes and towre aforefeid, as well workmen and laborers, as all manner of ftuffe and ordinaunces as fhall be required or neceffary for performance of the fame, except the feid Mr-Provoft, fcolers, and furveyor granten to lend to the feid John Waftell fum part of old fcaffoldyng tymbre, and the ufe of certayne ftuffe and neceffaryes there, as gynnes, whels, cables, hobynatts, fawes, and fuch other as fhall be delyvered to him by indenture, and the feid John Waftell to delyver the fame agayne unto the feid fuveyor as fone as the feid buttraffes and towre fhall be performed The feid John Waftell graunteh alfo and byndeth himfelf by thefe covenauntes to perform and clerely fynyfh all the feid buttraffes and towre on this fide the fteerle of the Annunciation of our Bleffed Lady next enfuyng after the date hereof And for the good and fuer performyng of all thefe premyffes, as is afore fpecyfyed, the feid Provoft and fcolers covenaunten and granten to paye unto the feid Waftell for the performyng of evry buttraffe 6l 13s 4d which amownteth for all the feid buttraffes 140l and for performyng of the feid towre 100l to be paid in forme followyng, That is to fey, from tyme to tyme as moche money as fhall fuffile to pay the mafons and other laborers rately after the numbre of workmen, and alfo for fton at fuche tymes and in fuche forme as the feid John Waftell fhall make his provyfion or receyte of the fame fton, from tyme to tyme as the cafe fhall requyre, provided alwey that the feid John Waftell fhall kepe continually 60 fre-mafons workyng upon the fame works, as fone as fhall be poffible for him to call them in

by

by vertue of fuche commiſſyon as the feid furveyor fhall de-
lyvre unto the feid John Waſtell for the fame entent, and in
cafe ony mafon or other laborer fhall be found unproſytable
or of ony fuche ylle demeanor whereby the work fhould be
hyndred or the company mifordered, not doing their duties
accordyngly as they ought to doo, then the feid furveyor to in
devor himfelf to performe tnem by fuche wayes as hath byn
there ufed before this tyme, And alfo the afore named Mr
Provoſt, fcolers, ard furveyor fhall fynde as moche iron work
for the fynvalls of tne feid buttrafles as fhall amounte to 5s.
fcr every buttraffe, that is in all 4l 5s And whatfoever
iron work fhall be occupied and fpent about the feid works
and for fuertie of the fame above the feid 5s for a buttraffe,
the feid John Waſtell to fee hytt at his own coſt and charge,
And for all and fingu'er covenauntes afore reherfed of the
partye of the feid John Waſtell wele and truly to be perform
ed and kepte, he byndeth himfelf, his heirs and executors in
3col of good ard lawfulle money of Englande to be paid unto
the feid Mr Provoſt, fcolers and furveyor at the ffeefte of
Lffer nxt comyng after tne date of thes prefentes, And in
lyke wife for all and finguler covenauntes afore reherfed of
the partye of the feid Provoſt, fcolers and furveyor wele and
truly to be performed and kepte, they bynde them their fuc
ceffors and executors in 300l. of good and lawfulle money of
Englande to be paid unto the feid John Waſtell at the feid
ffeefte of Efter, in witneffe whereof the partyes aforefeid to
ths prefent indenture interchangeably have fett their feales
the day and yere above wryten

The FOURTH INDENTURE.

Concerning four large Windows of Painted Glafs, af
ter the rate of fixteen pence per foot for the Glafs,
to be made after the manner ard goodnefs in every
point of the King's New Chapel at Weſtminſter,
alfo according to the manner done by Bernard Flower Clazier, deceafed, alfo according to fuch Patterns, otherwife called Vidimus *

* The Paintings of the Chapel Windows were (as we may
reafonably imagine, copied from the juft pieces that could be col
lected from all quarters. The patterns from which the figures
er

THIS INDENTURE made the thirde day of the moneth of May in the yere of the reigne of Herry the 8th by the Grace of God Kyng of Englande and Fraunce, Defendor of the Fteyth and Lorde of Ireland the eightene, betwene the Right Worshepfulle masters Robert Hacombleyn Doctor of Divinitie and Provost of Kynge's college in the universitie of Cambrydge, William Holgylle clerke master of the hospitalle of Seint John Baptiste called the Savoy besydes London, and Thomas Larke clerke Archdeacon of Norwyche on that oon partye, and Ffraunces Wylliamson * of the paryshe of Seint Olyff in Southwerke in the countie of Surrey glasyer, and Symond Symonds * of the paryshe of Seint Margaret of the towne of Westminster in the countie of Middlesex, on that other partye, witnesseth, That it is covenaunted condescended and aggreed betwene the seid partyes by this indenture in manner and forme folowing, that is to wete, the seid Ffraunces Wylliamson and Symond Symonds covenaunte, graunte and them bynde by these presentes that they shalle at their owne propre costes and charges wele, surely, clenely, workmanly, substantyally curyously and sufficyently glase and sett up or cawse to be glased and sett up foure windowes of the upper story of the grete churche within the kynge's college of Cambrydge, that is to wete, two wyndowes on the oon side of the seid churche, and the other two wyndowes on the other side of the same churche with good, clene, sure and perfyte glasse and oryent colors and imagery of the story of the old lawe and of the newe lawe after the forme, maner, goodnefs, curyousity, and clenelyness in evry poynt of the glasse wyndowes of the Kynge's newe chapell at Westminster , And also accordyngly and after suche maner as oon Barnard Fflower

*n the glass were traced, is in the indenture termed a Vidimus

' ' As much as we imagine ourselves arrived at higher perfection in the arts, it would not be easy for a master of a college now to go into St Margaret s parish, or Southwark, and bespeak the roof of such a chapel as that of King's college, and a dozen or two of windows so admirally drawn, and order them to be sent home by such a day, as if he was bespeaking a chequered pavement, or a church bible Even these obscure Artifts Williamson, Symonds, Flower, Hoone, &c would figure as considerable painters in any reign and what a rarity, in a collection of drawings, would be one of their Vidimus s '

Walpole s Anec. on Painting.

Fflower glafyer late deceafed by indenture ftode bounde to doo , And alfo accordyng , to fuche patterns otherwyfe called vidimus, as by the feid mafters Robert Hacombleyn, William Holgylle and Thomas Larke or by ony of them to the feid Ffraunces Wylliamfon and Symond Symondes or to eitner of them fhall be delyvered, for to forme glaffe ard make by the forefeid foure wyndowes of the feid churche , Aid the feid Ffraurces Wylliamfon and Symiond Symoides, covenaunte and graunte by thefe prefentes that two of the feid wyndowes fhall be clerely fett up and fully fynyfhed after the forme abovefeid within two yeies next enfuyng after the date of thefe prefentes, and that the two other wyndowes refydue of the feid foure wyrdowes fhall be clerely fett up and full, fynyfhed within the veres next enfuyng after that ————without any furuer or longer delay Furdermore the feid Ffraunces Wylliamfon and Symond Symondes covenaurte and graunte by thefe prefentes taat they fhall ftrongely and furely bynde all the feid foure wyndowes with double bares of leade for defence of great wyndes and other outraci cus weih , Aid the feid mafters Robert Hacombleyn, William Holgylle and Thomas Larke covenaunte and griunte by thefe prefentes, that the feid Ffraunces Wylliamfon and Symond Symondes fhall have for the glaffe, workmanffip and fettyng up of every ioot of the feid glaffe by them to be provide , wrought and fett up after the forme abovefeid ix tene perce fterlinges , And where the feid Ffraunces Wyl hamfon and Symond Symondes, aid Ho John a Mere of m par, ie of Seint Margaret of the towne of Weftmynfter ia the countie of Middlefex, fquyer, John Kellet of t e fame paryfhe owne and coure, yoman Garrard Meynes of de paryfhe of Seint Oliffe in Southwerke in the countie of Su rey, joyner, and Henry Johnfon cf the paryffhe of Seint Cle ment Dates without the barres of the newe temple ol Loncon in the countie of Middlefex, cordwaner, by their wryttyng obligatory of the date of thefe prefentes be holden and bouide to the feid maters Robert Hacombleyn, William Holgylle and Thomas Larke in the fumme of two handied poundes fter linges to be paid at the ffeefte of the Nativitee of Seint John Baptifte now nextcomyng after the date of their prefentes, as in the fame wryttyng obligatory more plainly at large dootne appere Neverthelefle the fame maiters Robert Hacombleyn, William Holgylle and Thomas Larke for them and their exe cutors covenaunte and graunte by thefe prefentes, that yf the

feid

feid Ffraunces Williamfon and Symond Symondes on their
part wele and truly performe, obferve, fulfille and kepe all
and evry the coverauntes, bargaynes, grauntes, and promyfes
and agreements afore'eid in maner and forme as is above declared, That then the fame writtvng obligatory fhall be voyd
and had for nought, and elfe it fhall ftande in fulle ftrengthe
and effect   In witneffe whereof the feid partyes to thefe indentures interchangeably have fett their feals

Yoven the day and yere abovefeid.

The FIFTH INDENTURE. *

Concerning fixing up eighteen Windows of painted
Glafs (among which is numbered the Weft Window) like thofe of the King's new Chapel at Weftminfter, as Bernard Flower, glazier (late deceafed)
ftood bound to do, fix of the faid Windows to be
fet up within twelve months   The glafs to be after
the rate of fixteen pence per foot · the lead two
pence per foot.

THIS INDENTURE made the lafte day of the moneth
of Aprelle in the yere of the reigne of Herry the 8th
by the grace of God Kyng of England and Ffraunce, Defendor of the Ffeyth and Lorde of Ireland the eightene, betwene the Right Worfhepfulle Mafters Robert Hacombleyn
Doctor of Divinitie and provoft of the Kynge's college in the
univerfitie of Cambrydge, mafter William Holgylle clerke
mafter of the hofpitalle of Seint John Baptifte called the Savoy
befydes London, and mafter Thomas Larke clerke archdeacon of Norwyche on that oon partye, and Galyon Hoone of
the paryffh of Seint Mary Magdelen next Seint Mary Overey
in Suthwerke in the countie of Surrey glafyer, Richard
Bownde of the paryffh of Seint Clement Danes without the
barres of the newe temple of London in the countie of Middlefex, glafyer, Thomas Reve of the paryffh of Seint Sepulcre
without

---

*The fourth and fifth Indentures give an account of the
glazing of twenty-two Windows The four remaining Windows, which were not fet up by the glaziers fpoken of in the Indentures, are, as I am led to believe, the three Windows that feem
inexplicable, and the Weft Window.

without newgate of London, glafyer, and James Nicholfon
of Seint Thomas Spyteil or Hofpitalle in Southwerke in the
countie of Surrey glafyer, on that other partye witneffeth,
That it is covenaunted condefcended and agreed betwene the
feid partyes by this indenture in manner and forme folowing,
that is to wete, the feid Galyon Hoone, Richard Bownde
Thomas Reve and James Nicholfon covenaunte, graunte and
them bynde by thefe prefentes that they fhalle at their own
propre coftes and charges well, furely, clenely, workmanly,
fubftantially, curioufly and fufficiently glafe and fett up, or
caufe to be glafed and fett up eightene wyndowes of the
upper ftory of the great churche within the kynge's college
of Cambrydge, whereof the wyndowe in the efte ende of the
feid churche to be oon, and the wyndowe in the weft ende of
the fame churche to be another, And fo feryatly the refydue
with good, clene, fure and perfyte glaffe and oryent colors and
imagery of the ftory of the olde lawe and of the newe lawe
after the forme, maner, goodnefs, curioufytie, and clenely-
nef, in evry poynt of the glaffe wyndowes of the kynge's
newe chapeil at Weftminfter, and alfo accordyngly and after
fuche maner as oon Barnard Fflower glafyer lately deceafed by
indenture ftode bounde to doo, that is to fey, fix of the feid
wyndowes to be clerely fett up and fynyfhed after the forme
aforefeid within twelve moneths next enfuyng after the date
of thefe prefentes, And the twelve wyndowes refydue to be
clerely fett up and fully fynyfhed within foure yeres next en
fuyng after the date of thefe prefentes And that the feid
Galyon, Richard Thomas Reve, and James Nycholfon fhalle
fuerly bynde all the feid wyndowes with double bands of leade
for defence of great wyndes and outragious wetheringes,
Furdermore the feid Galyon, Richard, Thomas Reve and
James Nycholfon covenaunte and graunte by thefe prefentes
that they fhall wele and fufficiently fett up at their owne propre coftes and charges all the glaffe that now is there ready
wrought for the feid wyndowes at fuche tyme and whan as the
feid Galyon, Richard, Thomas Reve and James Nycholfon
fhall be affigned and appoynted by the feid mafters Robert
Hacombleyne, William Holgvile, and Thomas Larke or by
any of them, And wele and fufficiently fhall bynde all the
fyme with double bandes of leade for the defence of wyndes
and wetheringes, as is aforefeid after the rate of two pence
every ffootte, And the feid mafters Robert Hacombleyne,
William Holgylle and Thomas Larke covenaunte and graunte
by

by thefe prefentes, that the aforefeid Galyon, Richard Bownde Thomas Reve and James Nicholfon fhall have for the glaffe workmanfhip and fetting up twenty foot of the feid glaffe by them to be provided, wrought, and fett up after the forme abovefeid fixtene pence fterlinges , Alfo the feid Galyon Hoone, Richard Bownde, Thomas Reve and James Nichol-fon covenaunte and graunte by thefe prefentes that they fhall delyver or caufe to be delyvered to Frraunces Williamfon of the paryffhe of Seint Olvff in Southwerk in the countie of Surrey glafyer, and to Symond Symondes of the paryffhe of Seint Margaret of Weftminfter in the countie of Middlefex glafyer, or to either of them good and true patterns otherwyfe called a vidimus, for to forme glaffe and make by other four wyndowes of the feid churche, that is to fey, two on the oon fyde thereof and two on the other fyde, whereunto the feid Ffraunces and Symond be bounde, the feid Ffraunces and Symond paying to the feid Galyon, Richard Bownde, Thomas Reve and James Nicholfon for the feid patterns otherwyfe called a vidimus as moche redy money as fhall be thought reafonable by the forefeid mafters William Holgylle and Thomas Larke, And where the feid Galyon Hoone, Richard Bownde, Thomas Reve and James Nycholfon by their writing obligatory of the date of thefe prefentes be holden and bounden to the feid mafters Robert Hacombleyn, William Holgylle and Thomas Larke, in the fumme of five hundred markes fterlinges to be paide at the ffeefte of the nativitie of Seint John Baptifte now next coming after the date of thefe prefentes, as in the writtyng obligatory more plainly at large may appere , Neverthelesse the fame mafters Robert Hacombleyn, William Holgylle and Thomas Larke for them and their executors wille and graunte by thefe prefentes that yf the feid Galyon Hoone, Richard Bownde, Thomas Reve and James Nycholfon well and truly performe, obferve, fulfille and kepe all and evry the covenauntes, bargaynes, grauntes, promyfes and aggreements aforefeid in maner and forme as above declared, That then the feid writtyng obligatory fhall be voyde and had for nought, and elfe it fhall ftand in all ftrength and effect , In witneffe whereof the feid partyes to thefe indentures interchangeably have fett their feales.

Yoven the day and yere abovefeid.

M

✤✤✤
✤✤✤✤✤✤✤✤✤✤✤✤✤✤✤✤✤✤✤✤✤✤✤✤✤✤✤✤✤✤✤✤✤✤✤✤✤✤✤

A
SUPPLEMENT
TO THE
ACCOUNT of the WINDOWS.

THOUGH, in my account of the Paintings, I for-
bore dwelling on each particular ftroke of art,
and apologifed for the fame ; yet, left fuch an omif-
fion fhould be thought a defect, and expofe me to the
cenfure of my reader, I have employed fome pains
in pointing out the moft ftriking and admired beauties
of the Chapel-Windows ——The firft occur in

The Fourth Window.

The Queen of Sheba, &c.—The attitude of Sheba
has great merit

The Wife-men, &c —Remark the figure of the child
the flowing of Mary's drapery the pofture of one of the
Magi approaching Chrift with veneration · his countenance the richnefs of his mantle —A beautiful ftar
in the uppermoft part of the painting.

The Fifth Window.

The Purification, &c.—The face of the perfon who
is bearing Chrift in his arms, and the cage and doves
are far from being unworthy our notice.

Jacob, to avoid the fury &c —The countenance of
Ifaac bears an aged and venerable appearance *

Th

* *In the back-ground we often find the fame perfons in mi-
niature, that were the fubject of the principal painting —In the
back-ground, or upper part of this painting, we have a diffe-*
re

The Sixth Window.

The children of Israel, &c —The calf and pillar are frequently, and not undeservedly, admired.

Simeon blessing, &c — The beauty of this piece consists in the attitude and dress of Simeon.

Herod's cruelty, &c —A majestic figure of Herod on horseback But above all remark the merciless looks of the assassin, who is preparing to unsheath his sword against the naked infant at his feet.

The Seventh Window.

Naaman washing, &c —Naaman washing is not badly represented.

The Eighth Window

Elisha raising, &c —This whole piece is exceedingly noble. The building in it is well painted

Christ raising Lazarus, &c —The gesture of Lazarus, his pale and ghastly countenance, have each a peculiar beauty

David returning, &c.—The harp and the virgin bearing it are well figured

Christ riding, &c.—An earnestness in the looks of Zaccheus, whose eyes are stedfastly fixed on Christ, usually receives a particular applause

The

view of Jacob supposed to be far advanced on his journey —The same thing may be observed in the painting underneath, which represents Joseph and Mary travelling towards Egypt —But these, as well as some other circumstances which may chance to fall under my notice, I do not number among the most finished beauties . and, therefore, I would be understood to have mentioned them for this reason only,—lest any figures should escape a spectator's observation at an hasty view, which, if discerned, might yet conduce highly to his pleasure and satisfaction —If a beholder will allow himself time for a strict examination of the several paintings, he will find his trouble not ill repaid by a discovery of the nicest perfection in each particular piece.

The NINTH WINDOW.

Manna falling, &c —Moſes and Aaron make the beſt appearance in this piece ——Many have expreſſed no ſmall ſatisfaction at beholding the Manna

The laſt ſupper, &c —Chriſt giving the ſop to Judas Some are apt to imagine that they perceive in Judas a traiterous and deceitful look.

The TENTH WINDOW

Judas the firſt, &c.—Here again ſome obſerve the traitor in the countenance of Judas But let not the cheeks of the trumpeter in this painting eſcape a ſpectator's notice. which appear as if naturally diſtended with wind, and ſwelling from the glaſs —The terrified looks of the ſervant, whom Peter is ſmiting, canno be beheld with indifference.   t

Chriſt bound, &c —Every moment employed in viewing the meek and lowly figure of Jeſus, affords a freſh pleaſure to the ſight In the upper part of this painting is the figure of a woman executed in a maſterly manner.

The ELEVENTH WINDOW.

Jeremiah impriſoned, &c —The figure and dreſs of Jeremiah are happily and boldly executed

Chriſt a priſoner, &c —The angry countenance of the high Prieſt, the luſtre of the colouring of his robes,* the throne on which he is ſeated, the coſtly canopy ſpread above it, the ill-favoured aſpect of a man ſtanding near our Saviour, and ſuppoſed to be ſaying " Anſwereſt thou the high Prieſt thus ?" are beauties with which a ſpectator may be highly entertained —Obſerve the dog.

Shimei curſing, &c —The impatient fury of Shimei (who is painted with a ſwarthy complexion) the downcaſt looks of David, with a certain conſciouſneſs of ſhame are by very judicious perſons pronounced almoſt inimitable

The

---

* *The richneſs and brightneſs of the* SCARLET *colour is every where conſpicuous.*

The foldiers mocking, &c —A kind of joy in the countenance of Herod, who expected some extraordinary interview, † is wonderfully well expressed —A curtain suspended over Herod's head is not without it's beauty.

The GRAND EAST WINDOW

Pilate pronouncing, &c.—The person of Pilate, the grandeur of the canopy hanging over him, and several countenances, that deserve somewhat more than a slight and momentary view, render this painting one of the most finished pieces about the Chapel.

Our Saviour bearing, &c —In our Saviour's face (who is almost fainting under the burden of his crofs) we may discern every possible mark of woe and anguish.

The stripping, &c.—Christ extended on the crofs, and the rough and stern visage of the smith, who is preparing for the use of his tools are just objects of admiration.

Christ crucified, &c.—Take particular notice of the ture of one of the soldiers (under the crofs) who is pointing to a die

The FOURTEENTH WINDOW

The lamentation of Mary, &c —An expression of sorrow and affliction in the face of Mary Magdalene is no contemptible stroke of art —But the mournful countenances of the women in the other painting of this Window, have not, perhaps, their parallels

The FIFTEENTH WINDOW.

Christ laid, &c —The features and lineaments of the face of the dead body of Christ are a most striking instance of the ability of the artist, who was employed about this piece

The passage of Christ, &c —Christ approaching the departed spirits in a descending posture, and the flowing of his garment (from his left shoulder) in strong and lively colours, are circumstances with which a spectator cannot but be exceedingly pleased.—In the upper part
of

† *Luke* xxiii 8.

of this painting are some figures intended for evil spirits, supposed to be flying from the sight of Christ.

The Sixteenth Window.

Christ, after that, &c —The figure of Christ rising from the sepulcre, and his flowing robe, are worth some little notice.

Jesus discovering, &c —Attend to the richness of Christ's robes, and the flowing of Mary's clothes.

The Seventeenth Window.

Reuben coming, &c —Reuben's dress can hardly fail of recommending itself to a spectator's observation.

The women going, &c —The painter seems, in this piece, to have exhausted the whole force of his art on the flowing of Mary Magdalene's gown, and on the beauty of it's colouring, which is blue —A very delicate and graceful figure of the Virgin Mary, with an head dress well suited to her person This latter observation may be extended to other representations of Mary above mentioned

Daniel in the lion's den, &c —Astonishment in the countenance of Darius is artfully expressed

Mary Magdalene mistaking, &c —The attitude of Mary, the folds of her garment, and the pales of the garden, are all exact copies of nature

The Eighteenth Window.

Christ appearing, &c —It is worth while to regard, how deep is the attention displayed in the countenances of one of the disciples.

Christ breaking, &c.—Marks of surprise in the whole mien of the two disciples cannot, I believe, escape the notice of the most ordinary beholder

The Twentieth Window

Elijah taken up, &c.—The mantle flowing down, the attitude of Elijah stooping down from the chariot, and the chariot itself, are all confessedly worthy of the highest admiration

Christ ascending, &c.—Christ disappearing, and the amazement of the beholders looking after him, make

up

up a lively reprefentation of what may be conceived
to have happened on fuch an occafion.

The Holy Ghoft, &c —A figure of the Virgin Mary
with an air of humility and devotion —I would recommend it to a fpectator to examine narrowly this
beautiful painting.

The TWENTY-FIRST WINDOW.

Peter and John, &c —This painting prefents us with
very remarkable beauties Such are the diftortion of
the cripple's knee (which does but feebly fupport him
in his endeavours to rife) apparently advancing out
from the glafs ; his countenance wan and meagre,
expreffive of want and mifery, and the magnificent
column of the temple.

The beggar reftored, &c —The group of diminutive
figures about Peter preaching, are delineated with exact tafte and judgment The number of them produces no confufion, nor yet a want of the moft eloquent
expreffions of attention in their countenances — This
Painting may be feen in an advantageous light from
the Organ-loft

The death of Ananias, &c.—" It is remarkable
" that one of the fineft of thefe windows is the ftory
" of Ananias and Saphira, as told by Raphael in the
" cartoons—probably the cartoons being configned
" to Flanders for tapeftry, drawings from them were
" fent hither · an inftance of the diligence of our
" glafs painters in obtaining the beft defigns for their
" work."   Walpole's Anec. on Painting.

The TWENTY-SECOND WINDOW.

The converfion, &c —The light fhining from Heaven
is very fuccefsfully executed.

Paul preaching, &c.—In the back-ground is an exceeding fmall figure of Paul let down by two men from
the top of a tower —Remark the attitude of the two
men —Thefe diminutive figures, though their extraordinary beauty is not eafily difcerned by the naked eye,
are

are reckoned by many people inferior to none about the Chapel.

The Twenty-Third Window.

I had thought to have taken no farther notice of any of the figures in the middle light, but an exceeding dignity in the looks of the uppermost Messenger in the lower division of this Window, obliges me to make mention of it as a new and uncommon beauty, and even equal to any already seen

The Twenty-Fourth Window

In the upper division of this Window, and in the light towards the left, about a yard from the bottom of the division, is painted the flame of a candle This single representation is coloured with such a masterly hand, that a spectator, while the sun is shining on the South side of the Chapel, may almost suffer himself to be deceived with the appearance,

THE END.

Lightning Source UK Ltd.
Milton Keynes UK
UKHW020645090223
416652UK00001B/44